EMOTIONAL INTELLIGENCE 2.0

MASTERY YOUR EMOTIONS, DEVELOP AND BOOST YOUR EI TO IMPROVE THE SKILL TO BUSINESS AND RELATIONSHIP

JENNIFER BRAUER

TABLE OF CONTENTS

INTRODUCTION

Our natural state of being, as one with our Soul, is a harmonious state of Love, in which the only feelings we have are of continuous peace and bliss. Therefore, if we are feeling any feeling other than peace and bliss, we have gotten out of balance somewhere. This is due to our conditioned and faulty thinking, which emerges as tolerations, needs and limiting beliefs. Using our Emotional Intelligence EIuips us to identify the message our Soul is sending us through these feelings, so we can rectify our thinking and thus move always towards Love.

It is almost certain you have heard of emotional quotient, EI, and emotional intelligence before, but have you ever asked yourself if you are emotionally intelligent? To go one step further, are you emotionally intelligent at work? What about as a leader? If you have pondered these questions, you may have also asked yourself why emotional intelligence is so important. In this article, I will share more about emotional intelligence and its importance to every person, every workplace, every society, and even to the entire world.

According to psychologists Peter Salovey and John Mayer, emotional intelligence is "the ability to perceive emotions, to access and generate emotions, to understand emotions and emotional knowledge, and to reflectively regulate emotions so as to promote emotional and intellectual growth." In layman's terms, it is the extent to which we are self-aware (able to recognize and understand our emotions), can self-manage (able to adapt and control our emotions and reactions), can motivate ourselves (taking the right actions to achieve a goal), can express empathy for other people, and possess strong social skills (ability to build positive relationships with others).

Emotional intelligence is measured through standardized tests and the result of these tests is called the Emotional Quotient (EI). The higher your EI is the better. However, unlike the Intelligence Quotient (IQ), which is often fixed by the time you reach a certain age, most scholars and psychologists believe EI is malleable and can be enhanced and learned.

WHAT IS EMOTIONAL INTELLIGENCE?

Emotional intelligence is the ability to become aware about our emotions, create and access the emotions and manage our emotional wealth so we can encourage our personal, professional and spiritual growth. The benefit is if you are completely aware of your emotions and control your actions and reactions, you can easily self-motivate as well as motivate everyone around, thus developing strong rapport and social skills with others and also express compassion for others.

20th century displayed the substance of IQ (Intelligence Quotient), and people's character was judged on the basis of their intelligent quotient. In layman's language, the ability to become a money spinner and attain every luxury possible.

Various researches have suggested it is a failed exercise. To lead a happy, prosperous and successful life emotional intelligence is rEIuired. Although intelligent quotient is measured under certain parameters such as mental age and chronological age, but emotional intelligence has no such parameters and can be enhanced at any stage of life.

Emotion and intelligence are two terms that are combined more as time passes. Many people have an innate ability to utilize the strengths of human nature to further success. Individuals with a high level of emotional intelligence have an insightful understanding of themselves and others. If a situation invokes stress, the person with a high level of emotional intelligence has

an instinctive ability to console and comfort another person.
Individuals with high levels of emotional intelligence can easily empathize with others. They see the situation from another person's perspective without stress. While some people are born with abnormally high levels of emotional intelligence, it is a trait the majority of people can learn. There are a myriad of benefits to EI encouragement. Individuals with high emotional intelligence are noted to achieve better results in projects. They can develop greater professional networks and achieve higher productivity.

Experts today cite many benefits to having a high level of EI. EI is usually measured by using four different areas of ability. The first level is that of general perception. What emotions are others feeling? People with a strong EI can detect the presence of emotion in themselves and others. They can often spot minor emotional problems that might lead to serious issues in the future.

The next area of measurement is that of using emotions. High EI often indicates a unique ability for problem solving and decision making. These cognitive traits are beneficial in the work environment. Experts have stated that emotional intelligence is the most important form of intelligence in the workplace. It is a natural process of motivation and problem management.

The third area of measurement in emotional intelligence is that of just understanding emotions. Human communication involves many forms of non-verbal language. People with high EI are capable of reading this emotional language in others. They are not intimidated by complicated relationships and can easily mediate disagreements. High EI individuals can coach positive emotions in co-workers and associates. They are wonderful motivators with a genuine and sincere enthusiasm. They are good at goal setting and can direct a group towards achievable and rewarding project conclusions.

The final area of testing for EI is that of managing emotions.

This is the ability to bring out the most positive and constructive emotions in everyone. Those with the ability to manage emotions can often overlook their negative feelings and maintain focus on goals and the necessary positive emotions to achieve them. EI-oriented individuals can gauge their own reactions and behaviors. This helps them see what influence their behaviors have on others before acting.

Emotional intelligence is a practical necessity in any office setting. The intensive self-reflection involved open communication with others. High EI individuals can achieve much more through self-awareness of goals and limitations. Because so many professions involve team atmospheres, emotional intelligence is a productive and beneficial element to the workplace.

People with high EI are frEIuently motivators. They are capable of understanding their personal moods and drives. They are EIually capable of understanding the same qualities in others. They can urge fellow employees or teammates to strive for the best work possible. A person with high emotional intelligence has a strong ability to control or change negative feelings. They naturally think prior to behaving on an impulse.

Emotional Intelligence consists of five basic components namely self-awareness, self-regulation, motivation, empathy and social skills. The first three competencies are intra-personal and concern your ability to know and manage yourself. Empathy and social skills are inter-personal competencies and concern your ability to interact and get along with others. The better your intra-personal skills, the easier it becomes to express your inter-personal skills. Mastering these skills will allow you to live a better, happier and more successful and fulfilled life.

Self-awareness is the first component of emotional intelligence. It is the ability to know which emotions you are feeling and why. When you understand your emotions, it is easier for you to acknowledge and control your emotions and prevent your feelings from ruling you. You also become more confident as you do not let your emotions get out of control. Being self-aware also enables you to take an honest look at yourself and you can better know your strengths and weaknesses, and work on these areas to achieve better outcomes for yourself and others.

Self-Regulation is the ability to control your emotions and impulses and choose the emotions you want to experience instead of being the victim of whatever emotions arise. When you are able to manage your emotional state, it becomes easier for you to think before you act and this prevents you from making impulsive and careless decisions. This skill also allows you to transform negative exhausting emotions into more positive and productive ones

The third component of emotional intelligence is motivation. This is about using your emotions to remain positive, optimistic and persistent rather than being negative and pessimistic. When you have a high degree of emotional intelligence you tend to be very motivated, productive and efficient in everything you do. You also use your emotions positively to take the right actions to persist and achieve your goals even in the face of considerable adversity or difficulty.

Empathy is the fourth element of emotional intelligence. It is the ability to truly recognize and understand the feelings and point of view of people around you. Empathetic people usually possess the ability to listen effectively and accurately to others and are normally excellent at managing relationships, improving communication, building trust and relating to others.

The fifth component of emotional intelligence is social skills. Emotionally intelligent people have good social skills and are excellent at building and maintaining relationships. When you are highly emotionally intelligent, you no longer focus on your own success first and you always have other's best interests in mind. You always promote an environment where people cooperate with each other instead of compete with one another and you always help others develop and grow.

Emotional intelligence is a key to success in life and the good news is whatever your actual level of emotional intelligence, you can improve it The best way to develop your emotional skills is through practice. You can then become more efficient at recognizing and managing your emotions as well as the emotions of others and lead a happier, more successful and fulfilled life.

Always remember the wise words of Daniel Goleman who said, "What really matters for success, character, happiness and lifelong achievements is a definite set of emotional skills - your EI - not just purely cognitive abilities that are measured by conventional IQ tests."

HOW EMOTIONAL INTELLIGENCE WAS DISCOVERED

The concept of emotional intelligence was brought to the public's attention by accident. The discoverers were two university professors that serendipitously faced the problem of managing emotions. These were Peter Salovey, a psychologist at Yale University and expert in emotions, and John Mayer, a psychologist at the University of New Hampshire. Being collaborators in research projects related to emotions, intelligence and personality; the two were also friends.

At that time, they were both enthusiast about a presidential candidate named Gary Hart because he was young and intelligent and promised to bring fresh perspectives. He was seen as a winner since he was endowed with essential qualities. However, the course of events was overturned by a shocking and unbelievable happening. When the candidates were running in the primaries, a reporter interviewed Gary Hart and confronted him about the so-called extramarital affair that rumors claimed he was having.

Hart launched a very bold and defiant answer by means of which he not only denied the allegations, but also dared the reporters to put him under surveillance. The exact words were:

"Follow me around. I don't care. I'm serious. If anybody wants to put a tail on me, go ahead. They'll be very bored." And the reporters took up the challenge so that within 24 hours from Hart's statement the Miami Herald laid down the story of his now-famous affair with Donna Rice.

The two professors were taken aback by the unfortunate gesture made by Gary Hart. They couldn't understand how such an intelligent man could commit such a gross and stupid mistake. Under these circumstances, the professors reached the conclusion that Hart, although very skilful in one area (political policy), lacked intelligence in another one, namely management of emotions.

Hence resulted the idea there must be another type of intelligence apart from cognitive intelligence. These two were separate and Peter Salovey and John Mayer decided to find methods of measuring the new type of intelligence discovered by them just as the cognitive intelligence was assessed. They further developed the concept of emotional intelligence and presented in a paper entitled in the same way, which was then published in a rather obscure scientific journal.

WHY IS EMOTIONAL INTELLIGENCE IMPORTANT?

EI may not be as well-known as IQ, yet many experts deem it as being more important than IQ. Why? Studies show EI is a better predictor of success, quality of relationships, and happiness of a person. It is evident everywhere and is critical in all aspects of life. Have you ever heard someone make statements like these: "Wow, what a positive person? He will surely achieve something great in life!" or "She is very caring and sociable. She is such a great boss." These comments illustrate that when a person has high EI (even when the person does not know it); it is seen and felt by others. It is these types of individuals who others tend to believe will most likely attain success. So, why is EI important to everyone?

1. EI is absolutely an important part of forming, developing, maintaining, and enhancing personal relationships with others. It is undeniable that people who know how to build positive relationships with other people will most likely be successful in their fields. Workers with high EI can work harmoniously in teams and adjust to changes. No matter how intelligent you are, if you have low emotional intelligence, you may find the path to success a struggle. However, there is good news. Take comfort in knowing you can improve your EI skills at any age and

regardless of past behavior.

2. Being aware of oneself means being able to handle constructive criticisms. You would probably agree there is no perfect person in the world and in everything we do, we need other people's criticisms and communication to do better. If you have a high EI, you are self-aware, meaning you understand your strengths, admit your weaknesses, and understand how your actions will affect other people surrounding you. Your high EI allows you to take these criticisms as an opportunity to improve your performance. This is a crucial part of working in an environment with many stakeholders.

3. Self-motivated people can inspire everyone. When a person is self-motivated, others around them often evaluate their own level of motivation. A self-motivated person is optimistic and is driven by what really matters to him/her. Who wouldn't want a self-motivated person around, right? Motivation is contagious and a highly-motivated household, workplace, or society will repeatedly outperform non-motivated ones. Low-motivation may be a sign your emotional quotient is low in one or more of the key EI quadrants.

4. EI makes the world genuine. People with a high Emotional Quotient have compassion that allows them to connect with others on an "emotional level." If a person is able to empathize with others, then he/she will work genuinely and attend to others' needs with compassion and care; even during times of challenge.

5. Having a high EI means being able to control yourself in all situations. Your fellow employee shouts at you angrily for some unknown reason. Given this scenario, would you be able to control your emotions and not act the same way he did? You see, EI is connected to how we control both our positive and our negative emotions. Think back to some of the decisions in your life you are not proud of. Ask yourself how many of them related to a lack of self-control or a lack of impulse control? The answer may be surprising.

Do you have greater clarity around what emotional intelligence and emotional quotient are? Do you agree it is more important than being "book-intelligent" or having a high IQ? Can you see why EI is the key to success? I refer to emotional intelligence as the missing link. You know it when you see it... even if you cannot identify it. The challenge is when emotional intelligence is missing it is not always easy to identify. It is often clear that a problem exists, but exactly what the problem is may be a mystery.

Knowing what you know about emotional intelligence I have a challenge for you. Ask yourself this question: are you an emotionally intelligent person at home and at work? If the answer is yes, you are on the right track! Continue along this path, strengthening your EI skills as you go, and you could be well on your way to success. If your answer is no, do not worry. Emotional intelligence is a set of skills you can improve with focus and a sound strategy. Regardless of where you are today, you cannot go wrong investing in yourself and improving your emotional intelligence skills.

THE FEATURES OF EMOTIONAL INTELLIGENCE

Emotional intelligence (EI) is the ability to identify and manage your emotions, as well as other people's emotions.
If you're emotionally intelligent you have the ability to:
Identify what you're feeling
Know how to interpret your emotions
Understand how your emotions can impact others
Regulate your own emotions
Manage other people's emotions
Some people naturally inherit high EI, but it's a skill you can practice and develop. By practicing emotionally intelligent behaviors your brain will adapt to make these behaviors automatic and replace less helpful behaviors.

1. Self-awareness
Self-awareness is the ability to accurately recognize your: emotions, strengths, limitations, actions and understand how these affect others around you.

Benefits:
Increases the likelihood of you handling and using constructive feedback effectively.

By knowing your strengths and weaknesses you can improve your organization's performance. For example, you may hire individuals who perform well in areas you struggle with.

Improve self-awareness by:

Keeping a diary of the situations that have triggered disruptive emotions in you, such as anger, and your thoughts and behaviors during those situations. With this information you can form an understanding of your emotions and reactions and work towards self-regulation.

Receiving feedback from staff, as this can highlight how others perceive you and it also helps you target unhelpful reactions.

Observing the response others have to your behavior.

2. Self-regulation

Self-regulation allows you to wisely manage your emotions and impulses - you show or restrain certain emotions depending on what is necessary and beneficial for the situation. For example, rather than shouting at your employees when you're stressed you may decide which tasks can be delegated.

Benefits:

Self-regulation helps earn the respect and trust of employees.

Useful when adapting to change.

Allows you to react rationally.

Improve self-regulation by:

Taking responsibility if you have made mistakes. Rather than blaming others admit that you are at fault. You'll feel less guilty and your team will respect you for it.

Responding to situations calmly as your communication is more effective when you're in this state and this feeling will spread to others. Breathing techniques, such as controlled breathing, can also be useful practice.

3. Empathy

To be empathetic means you are able to identify and understand others' emotions, i.e. imagining yourself in someone else's position.

Benefits:
Provides you with an understanding of how an individual feels and why they behave in a certain way. As a result, your compassion and your ability to help someone increase because you respond genuinely to concerns.
Especially helpful when delivering constructive feedback.
Being empathetic shows your team that you care. For example, if a manager reacts angrily after finding out an employee has been arriving to work late because their child is unwell, the team is likely to react negatively towards the manager. It would be more favorable for the manager to be understanding and agree on a plan of action with the employee, such as, the employee starting work earlier and finishing later.
Employees will respect you more and subsequently job performance will improve.

To develop empathy:
Imagine yourself in someone else's position. Even if you have not experienced a similar situation, remember a situation where you have felt the same emotion your employee is experiencing.
Practice listening to your employees without interrupting them.
Observe your employees and try to gauge how they're feeling.
Never ignore your employees' emotions, for example, if an employee looks upset don't disregard this - address it.
Try to understand first rather than form a judgment. For example, you may initially feel annoyed at an employee who seems cold and disinterested. However, after discovering they suffer from social anxiety you may feel more sympathetic.
To communicate your empathy keep your body language open and regulate your voice to show your sincerity.

4. Motivation

Being self-motivated consists of: enjoying what you do, working towards achieving your goals and not being motivated by money or status.

Benefits:
Reduces your likelihood of procrastinating
Increases self-confidence
Keeps you motivated even if you face setbacks
Makes you focused on achieving your goals
Spreads to the team
To increase your motivation:
Remember why you're doing your job - maybe think about why you wanted it initially.
Set new goals if you lack them.
Remain optimistic because to be motivated you must be positive. Even when there is a setback or a challenge identify one positive factor about it.
To increase your employees' motivation explain why they are valuable, using examples, as this will provide them with a sense of purpose.

5. Social skills
Effective social skills consist of managing relationships in a way that benefits the organization.

Benefits:
Effective social skills help you to build rapport with your employees and earn their respect and loyalty.
Employees will trust you, which is especially valuable if unwelcomed decisions have been made, such as a rise in performance targets.
When you interact with your employees you can identify the best way to meet their individual needs and identify how their abilities can be used to achieve the organization's aims.

Staff will feel comfortable presenting ideas to you and discussing concerns.

Improve social skills by:

Developing your communication skills. Problems can arise if there is bad communication, such as, misunderstandings upsetting employees.

Listen to feedback to work out what to target, for example, the manner in which you speak may need work or perhaps your body language.

Learning how to provide praise and constructive feedback.

Cooperating and working together with your employees because you are all working towards a shared goal.

Listening to employees and practicing empathy.

Building relationships with your employees will assist you in understanding how to manage each individual.

Resolving conflict by looking at the situation from all the viewpoints involved and tries to come to a compromise that benefits everyone.

SEGMENTATION OF EMOTIONAL INTELLIGENCE

1. Reflective Regulation of Emotions to promote Emotional and Intellectual Growth
• Ability to stay open to feelings, both those that are pleasant and those that are unpleasant.
• Ability to reflectively engage or detach from an emotion, depending upon how it's judged in formativeness or utility
• Ability to reflectively monitor emotions in relation to one's self and others, such as how clear, typical, influential, or reasonable.
• Ability to manage emotion in one's self and others by moderating negative emotions and enhancing pleasant ones without repressing or exaggerating information they may convey.

2. Understanding and analyzing Emotions; Employing Emotional Knowledge
• Ability to label emotions and recognize relations among the words and the emotions themselves, such as the relation between liking and loving.
• Ability to interpret the meanings that emotions convey

regarding relationships, such as that sadness that often accompanies loss.
• Ability to understand complex feelings: simultaneous feelings of love and hate, or blends, such as awe as a combination of fear and surprise.
• Ability to recognize likely transitions among emotions, such as the transition from anger to satisfaction, or from anger to shame.

3. Emotional Facilitation of Thinking
• Emotions prioritize thinking by directing attention to important parts of the information.
• Emotions are sufficiently vivid and available and can be generated as aids to judgment and memory concerning feelings.
• Emotional moods swings change the individual perspective from optimistic to pessimistic, encouraging consideration of multiple points of view.
• Emotional states differentially encourage specific problem approaches such as when happiness facilitates inductive reasoning and creativity.

4. Perception Appraisal and Expression of Emotion
• Ability to identify emotion in one's physical state, feelings and thoughts.
• Ability to identify emotions in other people, design, art work, etc., through language, sound, appearance and behavior.
• Ability to express emotion accurately and to express needs related to feelings.
• Ability to discriminate between accurate and inaccurate, or honest vs. dishonest expressions of feelings.

The other side of the concept also includes EI as a type of social intelligence that involves the ability to monitor one's own and others' emotions, to discriminate among them and to use the information to guide one's thinking and actions.

However, it stated that EI is actually a constellation of abilities, skills and dispositions which, which when taken together, can predict a person's likelihood of future success in a number of areas, including one's ultimate niche in society. This collection includes (but is not limited to) leadership, the ability to nurture relationships and keep friends, the ability to resolve the conflicts and skill at social analysis.

Subsequently, EI is mixed with the interpersonal and intrapersonal intelligence. Interpersonal intelligence is the ability to understand other people: what motivates them, how they work and how to work collectively. Whereas intrapersonal intelligence is a correlative ability turned inwardly. It is a capacity to form an accurate model of one's self and to be able to operate that model effectively in reality.

The key of EI is to use your emotions intelligently; you intentionally make your emotions work for you by using them to help guide your behavior and thinking in ways that enhance your results.

CHARACTERISTICS OF EMOTIONAL INTELLIGENCE

First of all it is important for you to understand the fact that your emotions impact various aspects of your daily life - the way you carry yourself, the way you behave and the way you interact with others. With a high EI you are capable of recognizing your own emotional state and that of the others. This understanding helps you to communicate and convince others in a way that draws them closer to you. The success with which you are able to use your EI leads to success in every path of your life, thus leading to more contentment in life.

Self-awareness: Did you ever stop to think who you really are inside? Whether you are good or bad, clever or dull, witty or serious, etc.? Well, when you sit in a place and observe yourself as an outsider you may be able to understand the real 'you'. When you examine yourself deeply you may understand why you acted in certain ways under certain circumstances.

The ability to examine yourself is called self-awareness. Self-awareness helps you identify your thoughts, actions, feelings, values, fears, shortcomings, strengths and overall the total 'you'. Besides yourself you can approach your loved ones and friends to help you to understand yourself. You can get a feedback from those who will give you their honest opinion of you. This helps to a certain extent to see how others perceive you.

In marketing this is done through a questionnaire about a company's product and performance. This is evaluated and used in improving the company's products and services. In the same way you could ask your loved ones to evaluate you and from their answers you could understand and improve your EI in areas where you are lacking.

As an adult you could do this exercise in the form of a journal. In fact, journaling is a great way to see the real you and your genuine feelings. You are more in tune with your own feelings when you have a high EI. This in turn increases your self-confidence in life, in dealing with yourself as well as with others.

Self-management: Self-awareness leads to self-management. Self-management is all about controlling your emotions and actions. You control yourself from having impulsive behaviors. You develop openness, adaptability, achievement and optimism. How do you react to certain situations? Do you respond or react to people and situations? There is a slight difference between these two words, but in practice there is a great difference in their meanings.

Reaction and response play a significant role in EI. For example, if you have to wait in a long line on a busy day when the traffic is moving ever so slowly, do you get impatient? Do you scream at other drivers and honk your horn loudly or wait patiently for the traffic to clear? Do you react or respond to heavy traffic?

If you are impatient you are reacting to traffic in an emotional way. When you react you tend to lose reason. On the other hand, if you show patience you are responding and therefore, you are more understanding and thoughtful. After all, the traffic has to move on at some point! Self-management stands for adaptability, transparency, achievement and optimism.

Social awareness: Your self-awareness and self-management takes you to the next step of social awareness. You are open to understanding the needs, emotions and concerns of other people. You are able to pick up on emotional cues, feel relaxed socially, and recognize the power play in a group or organization. In order to develop your EI you need to see and feel what others feel by walking in their shoes.

People with excellent social awareness are said to be more service minded, have empathy and organizational awareness. These are the main traits associated with social awareness according to Daniel Goleman. Social awareness at its best is offering a natural response to people, and taking their situation and needs into account as much as possible. If you exhibit these qualities you can consider your EI to be high.

Relationship management: The final area you need to develop in raising your EI is that of relationship management. We can look upon this trait in connection with your profession. This is the aspect of your EI that enables you to succeed in inspiring other people and helping them to reach their full potential. It is also vital in negotiating successfully, resolving conflicts and working with others toward a shared goal. Your success in this final area is directly correlated to your success in the other three areas because management is all about successfully interacting with other people. At the end of the day isn't efficient management all about getting the work done?

Aspects for a successful relationship management:
• Leadership - develop others by identifying their strengths; Influence others probably through your own motivation
• Communication - Being a change catalyst to incorporate new ideas when change is needed
• Conflict management - Connecting with people through networking
• Teamwork and collaboration- By giving credit to everyone to make them feel good about their own contribution.

How does Emotional intelligence affect your life?

Performance at work - EI helps you to comfortably handle social complexities of workplace, motivate and guide others and succeed in your career. Now-a-days companies view emotional intelligence as being an important aspect and perform EI testing before hiring.

Physical well-being - Stress is imminent in today's world no matter which profession you belong to. Stress is a familiar factor leading to serious health issues in most people. Uncontrolled stress level is known to increase the risk of heart disease. Our immune system suffers when stress levels are high.

Mental well-being - Stress affects mental health negatively. You might have read or heard about stressed people going to the extent of committing suicide. When you cannot manage your emotions you become a victim of mood swings or other mental disorders that can seldom allow you to form or maintain strong relationships in life.

Personal relationships - Understanding your emotions help you to express your feelings to your loved ones. When there is a block in communication your relationships suffer both at work and in your personal life.

Here are tips to increase your emotional intelligence:
• Learn to reduce negative emotions
• Stay cool and manage stress
• Be assertive and express difficult emotions when necessary
• Stay proactive, not reactive in difficult situations
• Bounce back from adversity
• Express intimate emotions in close, personal relationships

If you prefer you may write these done as different tips and post them in places where you can see them so you can incorporate them into your daily life.

Emotional Intelligence (EI) is an art to be developed in these times in order to intelligently tackle your emotions in every situation in life. This ability paves the way for success and self-satisfaction in every sphere of your life.

THE ELEMENTS OF EMOTIONAL INTELLIGENCE

Intellect and emotional intelligence are very different things. The former is the cognitive ability to synthesize and analyze data; to problem-solve and make associations based on available information. The latter is a set of innate and learned skills which facilitate relationships and enable a person to negotiate more easily through all areas of life.

Intellect can be measured by standardized IQ tests but there is no actual measure of the "EI," or Emotional Quotient. Even without a test. Its obvious when someone has a high IQ and it's just as obvious when someone has a high EI. Rather than try to measure it, though, it's more useful to look at the various elements that go into emotional intelligence.

While the IQ remains stable over a person's lifetime, the EI can be developed. Acquiring and practicing the following elements will enable you to boost your EI.

The first element of emotional intelligence is empathy. The ability to understand what other people are feeling will make you more sensitive and aware and will result in more meaningful relationships.

The second element is the recognition that your actions have consEIuences. This understanding will enable you to make conscious choices in your life and to avoid unnecessary difficulties.

Third on the list is good judgment. The gift of making well-thought-out decisions and seeing people for who they really are will maximize the possibilities of success in all areas of your life.

Number four is personal responsibility. When you hold yourself accountable and don't blame anyone else for your mistakes or misfortunes, you are empowered to change things for the better. Other people respect you, because you own up to your part in your relationships.

The fifth element is insight. The ability to see yourself clearly and to understand your own motivations allows for the possibility of personal growth. Insight into others allows you to have a greater impact in your relationships

Element number six is mental flexibility. Being able to change your mind or to see things from different points of view makes it possible for you to navigate all sorts of relationships and to succeed where other, more rigid thinkers would fail.

The seventh element is compassion. Being honest with yourself can be painful, but with a kind and gentle attitude, it's much easier. This type of compassion facilitates personal transformation, while compassion toward others supports deeper, more loving connections.

The eighth element is integrity. Following through on commitments and keeping your promises creates much good-will in personal and professional relationships and promotes success in both arenas.

Ninth on the list is impulse control. Thinking before speaking or acting gives you a chance to make deliberate, even sophisticated choices about how you present yourself to others. Not acting out of primitive impulses, urges or emotions avoids social embarrassment.

The tenth element is the ability to defer gratification. It's one thing to want something, but the ability to put off having it is empowering. Mastery of your needs allows you to prioritize around life goals.

Number eleven on the list is perseverance. Sticking with something, especially when it's challenging, allows you to see it through to completion and demonstrates to others you are dependable and potentially a high achiever.

The twelfth and final element is courage. Emotional courage (as opposed to the physical variety) is the ability to do the right thing, see the truth, open your heart and trust yourself and others enough to be vulnerable, even if all this is frightening. This causes others to hold you in high regard.

All these elements combine within you to make up your emotional intelligence. With a high EI, even a simple person is at an advantage in life. Without it, even someone with the most brilliant intellect is at a disadvantage.

REAL LIFE BENEFITS OF A HIGH
EMOTIONAL INTELLIGENCE

Most of us call it gut feeling, but now psychologists are calling those feelings emotional intelligence or EI. Emotional intelligence is something like your IQ. Your IQ score doesn't tell you how much you know, it simply tells you what your capacity to learn and comprehend is. Your EI is a tad trickier to measure and there is a great deal of disagreement on how it should be done. However, scientists can agree that in general, people who have a high EI, meaning they can identify their own emotions and the emotions of others, tend to have certain behaviors. Here's a quick list of some of those behaviors.

1. Adaptability
Developing emotional intelligence allows an individual to understand the emotions or motives of others and as a result they are more willing to adapt to a situation than a person who can only understand what they personally are feeling.

2. Managing emotions in others
Understanding the emotions in others is a key leadership trait which allows the person with high EI to influence others. Understanding needs and feelings lends itself to developing courses of action that will fulfill those needs and at the same

time accomplish what the leader wants accomplished.

3. Emotional control
Persons with a high EI understand their own emotions and can analyze them rationally. So when they experience frustration or fear or anger, they are less likely to react to them instinctively and are more likely to act in a controlled and informed manner.

4. Less Impulsive
High EI means bad news for marketers who depend on impulse buys. People with high EI don't react impulsively, but rather look at their feelings and make rational decisions without the interference of overwhelming emotional pull.

5. Strong relationships
Maybe one of the greatest advantages of elevated emotional intelligence is the ability to enter into and sustain strong and fulfilling relationships. Being able to understand and appreciate the emotions of others and not being driven by a "me first" need can result in more satisfying and less conflictive interactions with the people around you.

6. More optimistic
Face it. We live in a culture that sees the glass half empty more than we see it half full. High EI develops high self-esteem, which in turn gives the person the confidence to see the brighter side even in difficult situations.

7. Better stress management
Precisely because they have more self-esteem, self-confidence and an optimistic viewpoint of life, people with developed EI can handle more stress and pressure than others. Being able to identify stress points not as threats, but simply as challenges to be met, changes the nature of the stress to a manageable condition.

There are obvious advantages to developing emotional intelligence, but there are also arguments over how that can be done. Some say it is simply an innate skill you are born with. Others say you can improve it through training programs like emotional intelligence workshops. Whatever the answer is, it's obvious that understanding ourselves and the emotions of others has a distinct advantage in communications, relationships and personal behavior.

MYTHS ABOUT EMOTIONAL INTELLIGENCE

Myth: Emotional Intelligence just means being empathetic and understanding others' emotions.

Fact: Emotional Intelligence actually starts with self-awareness. Leaders with a strong EI will understand how to identify and regulate their own emotions, and they will also be adept at responding to others' emotions – whether that means bringing other people up or calming them down.

Myth: Emotional Intelligence is the most important indicator of professional success.

Fact: Although EI is a skill that's valuable in all fields, it's not the most important factor in long-term success. Functional/technical knowledge will always be a foundational rEIuirement for any job or industry. Where emotional intelligence comes in is knowing how to use technical skills in different environments, how to adapt to change, and how to motivate team members.

Myth: Emotional Intelligence is innate. You either have it or you don't.

Fact: While some people naturally have a stronger aptitude for social and emotional learning, emotional intelligence is learnable and actually develops naturally over one's lifetime. The earlier you begin learning to read nonverbal signals and understand conscious and unconscious motivations and biases, the more quickly you will develop and accelerate your EI and be able to harness it as a facilitation tool.

Myth: Emotional intelligence is a touchy-feely or feminine capacity:
Fact: This is not necessarily true. Going all the way back to ancient Greece, the ability to control or regulate your emotions has been perceived as a masculine trait. However, recent research shows than both men and women can lack emotional intelligence. Likewise, they can have it in abundance. They can also improve it at similar rates.

Myth: Emotional intelligence is only good for negotiating personal relationships:
Fact: This myth is perpetuated by personal gurus and life coaches who see people's inability to control their emotions in personal relationships as destructive to their overall well-being. However, EI is just as important in business as it is in your public life.

Myth: Emotional intelligence is primarily about being empathetic and caring for others' emotions:
Fact: EI is more about self-awareness than empathy.
For instance, a leader with good EI can negotiate an emotionally-charged situation, both controlling their own emotions and diplomatically responding to others' emotionally volatile behavior.

Myth: Emotional intelligence predicts whether or not someone will be a success in life:
Fact: This misconception was generated by the craze over EI, whereby people thought of it as a panacea for all life's problems. While EI is helpful in life, it's not the only ingredient

for success. For instance, some people with high IQ, as well as the ability to comprehend highly technical and abstract problems (think engineers and professors), tend to have low EI. They can be highly successful in life. But they are not considered ideal for management or leadership positions.

FACTS ABOUT EMOTIONAL INTELLIGENCE

Emotional and social skills are four times more important than IQ when considering success and prestige in professional settings. Different studies give different results. However, in a study of PhDs, social and emotional intelligence was significantly more important to professional success and prestige than IQ alone.

We learn (and can unlearn) emotions. Not only do children learn how to distinguish emotions in themselves and others, they learn how to experience and react to emotions and channel their natural temperaments.

Through limbic resonance, our bodies feel other people's emotions. "Emotions are contagious. We catch them and we spread them."

Emotions guide every decision we make.

By changing our bodies, we can change our emotions. Research on liking, alertness and confidence indicate people change attitudes and responses based on changes in their bodies. In addition, changing our bodies can change our own sense of power and even body chemistry.

We are always experiencing some sort of emotion...even when we try to be emotionless. We may not show an emotion, but the fact our bodies secrete hormones and we are interpreting the world around us causes us to perceive the world, assess it and experience a sensation –feel an emotion.

Emotions affect our health, our relationships and our financial well-being. How we respond to other people and events in our lives often determines how people respond to us. The course of our lives often depends on our level of emotional intelligence (EI).

Mind, body, language and emotion are all tied together. The mind-body connection is nothing new. However, research on the effect of emotions on the body is intriguing. This article shows how the physical body changes to reflect different emotions.

Emotions predispose us to act in particular ways. If we are angry, we see the world in a way that reinforces that anger and causes us to act differently than if we are fearful, sad or deliriously happy.

Emotional intelligence can be learned. Through a process called "plasticity," the brain changes as individuals practice new emotional intelligence strategies.

Your EI can help you improve your public image. A study of malpractice lawsuits showed surgeons who spent an extra 3 minutes comforting and being supportive towards their patients, were less likely to be sued.

The core of emotional intelligence is understanding of one`s emotions and emotional states of others. Unfortunately, only 36% of people can recognize their emotions accurately and timely.

Even though women and men have Equal potentials for developing emotional intelligence, some slight differences can occur in the following: in adulthood, women tend to develop their empathy and social skills, while men have been predominantly oriented to self-regulation.

PROS AND CONS OF EMOTIONAL INTELLIGENCE

Emotional intelligence is a description of how well an individual is able to be in touch with their own feelings. People who are skilled in this trait are also very good at sensing how those around them are feeling. This information is then used to determine what the best course of action should be when a choice must be made. Up to 80% of the difference between an average performer and a top performer is the ability to use this skill.

What Are the Pros of Emotional Intelligence?

1. It is something that anyone can learn.
Emotional intelligence isn't a genetic trait or a natural talent. It is a skill anyone can learn. Of course there will be some folks who are naturally better at learning this skill than others, but anyone has the potential to develop well-defined skills in this area. As long as you're willing to put in the practice, you'll be able to find some success.

2. It can help to reduce bullying.
When we understand our emotions and can tap into the emotions of others, then we get to feel a little bit of what others

are feeling around us. This allows us to stay in better control of our own emotions, while at the same time it prevents us from causing harm to others because we'll be feeling that harm internally. The end result is typically a kinder, more caring environment because compassion becomes a top priority.

3. It improves a person's social effectiveness.
By understanding the emotions of everyone else around them, a person exercising their skills of emotional intelligence can find ways to relate to others at a core level. This helps to improve their interpersonal relationships and draw people closer to them in social situations because the emotional intelligence also increases the perception levels of those around the individual.

4. It reduces the likelihood of engaging in personally destructive behaviors.
People who have enhanced their emotional intelligence skills over time are less likely to engage in self-destructive behaviors. There are lower levels of smoking, binge drinking, violence against others, and illicit drug use in those with an above average emotional intelligence when compared to the general population. This is because the negative emotional impacts of these decisions have a greater emphasis.

5. Making decisions becomes a lot faster.
Emotional decisions are a lot easier to make than logical decisions. Logic dictates that every scenario be evaluated, estimated, and anticipated. Emotional decisions happen faster because only the emotions of the situation are being examined. Emotion is one of the most crucial pieces of information we have access to every day, so more data can actually be examined in an emotion than through logic and that's why decisions are faster.

6. It can be used in any environment, situation, and

circumstance.

If you have a skill in typing 140 words per minute, are you going to be able to translate that skill into carpentry? Long haul driving? Emotional intelligence is a skill that transcends industries, hobbies, and situations because it is always applicable. A person exercising their skills in this area can find a way to relate to anyone in any circumstance or situation.

What Are the Cons of Emotional Intelligence?

1. It can be used to manipulate people.

Emotions are one of the core components of our being. We experience emotions in virtually every moment of every day. When those emotions are understood as a skill, then it becomes another way to manipulate someone to do what you want them to do. A high emotional intelligence might eliminate physical bullying, but if the intentions are not good, then a different type of bullying can come about: emotional bullying. What's worse is that the person being bullied will want to have it happen because it is emotionally fulfilling for them.

2. It prevents others from using their critical thinking skills.

When someone knows how to "put their emotion on a plate," then that emotional exposure can help others relate through that contact. As those emotions are placed strategically into a presentation, speech, or other public arena, those who are hearing and feeling those expressed emotions begin to get emotional themselves. As those uncontrolled emotions increase, the amount of logical thinking decreases and this prevents critical thinking from occurring.

3. It can be used for personal gain.

Emotional intelligence can also be used to manipulate others for personal gain. This can be done through the creation of embarrassing situations or outright emotional lies, showing a person positive emotions while showing everyone else negative emotions. High emotional intelligence skills can definitely create a lot of good, but if the desires are self-serving, it can also create a lot of darkness.

4. It can make a person more open and agreeable.
Social factors are very important within the scope of human existence. Rare is the individual who can live on their own without any personal contact of any kind for an extended period of time. For those who have a high emotional intelligence, they tend to be more open and agreeable to situations that are morally questionable if it means there is the chance for social contact. This effect is even more pronounced when someone with a higher emotional intelligence is controlling the situation.

5. It takes time to develop this skill.
Although everyone can develop emotional intelligence skills, this is a time investment that can be quite extensive and personal. People may not wish to look at their fears and habits or other personalized negative emotions. If one isn't willing to look inward, then there isn't a chance to adapt to emotions that are outward.

6. Emotional intelligence is a skill that not everyone takes seriously.
Information is the primary currency today and society often separates emotions from words. After all, how many times can a Facebook post or a tweet on Twitter are taken out of context because it is taken the wrong way? This skill isn't taken seriously because many people have poor skills in this area in the first place. Misinterpreting someone's status updates is clear evidence of this fact.
The pros and cons of emotional intelligence show it can be hugely beneficial to develop. It also shows there can be some potentially dangerous situations that develop if people use their

emotional intelligence in a way that only benefits themselves. By understanding the core emotions of those around us, better decisions can be made, so as long as the negatives can be balanced properly, emotional intelligence will always be important.

EI VS. IQ

Emotional Intelligence, or emotional quotient (EI), is defined as an individual's ability to identify, evaluate, control, and express emotions. People with high EI usually make great leaders and team players because of their ability to understand, empathize, and connect with the people around them. IQ, or intelligence quotient, is score derived from one of several standardized tests designed to assess an individual's intelligence.

IQ is used to determine academic abilities and identify individuals with off-the-chart intelligence or mental challenges. EI is a better indicator of success in the workplace and is used to identify leaders, good team players, and people who best work by themselves.

EI versus IQ comparison chart

EI: Stands for Emotional Intelligence (aka emotional quotient)
IQ: Intelligence Quotient (IQ)
Emotional quotient (EI) or emotional intelligence is the ability to identify, assess, and control the emotions of one's self, of others, and of groups.

An intelligence quotient (IQ) is a score derived from one of several standardized tests designed to assess intelligence.

EI: Abilities Identify, evaluate, control and express emotions one's own emotions; perceive, and assess others' emotions; use emotions to facilitate thinking, understand emotional meanings.

IQ: Ability to learn, understand and apply information to skills, logical reasoning, word comprehension, math skills, abstract and spatial thinking, filters irrelevant information.

EI: In the workplace teamwork, leadership, successful relations, service orientation, initiative, collaboration.

IQ: Success with challenging tasks, ability to analyze and connect the dots, research and development.

EI: Identifies Leaders, team-players, individuals who best work alone, individuals with social challenges.

IQ: Highly capable or gifted individuals, individuals with mental challenges and special needs.

EI: Origin 1985, Wayne Payne's doctoral thesis "A Study of Emotion: Developing Emotional Intelligence" Popular use came in Daniel Goleman's 1995 book "Emotional Intelligence - Why it can matter more than IQ" 1883.

IQ: English statistician Francis Galton's paper "Inquiries into Human Faculty and Its Development" The first application came in French psychologist Alfred Binet's 1905 test to assess school children in France.

EI: Popular Tests Mayer-Salovey-Caruso Test (emotion-based problem-solving tasks); Daniel Goleman model Score (based on emotional competencies).

IQ: Stanford-Binet test; Wechsler; Woodcock-Johnson Tests of Cognitive Abilities.

What is EI?

Emotional intelligence is the "ability to validly reason with emotions and to use emotions to enhance thought." EI refers to an individual's ability to perceive, control, evaluate, and express emotions. People with high EI can manage emotions, use their emotions to facilitate thinking, understand emotional meanings and accurately perceive others' emotions. EI is partially determined by how a person relates to others and how they maintain emotional control.

What is IQ?

Intelligence quotient or IQ is a score received from standardized assessments designed to test intelligence. IQ relates directly to intellectual pursuits such as the ability to learn as well as understand and apply information to skill sets. IQ covers logical reasoning, word comprehension and math skills. People with a higher IQ can think in abstracts and make connections by making generalizations easier.

Can EI or IQ be enhanced?

Emotional awareness is best inculcated from an early age by encouraging qualities like sharing, thinking about others, putting one's self in another person's shoes, giving individual space and the general principles of cooperation. There are toys and games available to increase emotional intelligence, and children who do not do well in social settings are known to perform significantly better after taking SEL (Social and Emotional Learning) classes. Adult EI can also be enhanced, although to a limited extent through effective coaching.

There are some conditions like high functioning autism (HFA) or Asperger's where one of the symptoms may be low-empathy. While some studies have found that adults with Asperger's have low-empathy, there have been studies with control groups that indicate EI can be changed in individuals with HFA or Asperger's.

IQ is more of a genetic make, but there are several ways to raise an individual's IQ to its highest potential through brain-food and mental ability exercises like puzzles, lateral thinking problems, and problem-solving techniques that make you think outside the box.

Applications

For a long time, IQ was believed to be the ultimate measure for success in careers and life in general, but there are studies that show a direct relation between higher EI and successful professionals. People with high EI generally achieve more, excel at teamwork and service and take more initiative. Several corporations and large organizations have mandated EI tests during the hiring process, and have coaching seminars on emotional and social skills. Social and Emotional Learning (SEL) is gaining a lot of popularity not only with professionals, but also among students.

IQ tests are used mostly in the fields of education and psychology. IQ tests are standardized to recognize highly capable/gifted individuals, as well as individuals who need special assistance in the classroom. IQ predicts success with academic achievements, and has often been used to determine career options for graduating students.

Measurement and Testing

Although measuring EI is very subjective, there are several standardized tests that measure emotional intelligence. Mayer-Salovey-Caruso Emotional Intelligence Test puts testers through a series of emotion-based problem-solving questions. The score reflects a person's capacity for reasoning with emotional information. Goleman's model of measurement focuses on emotional competencies. Goleman's model utilizes one of two tests: the Emotional Competency Inventory or the Emotional Intelligence Appraisal. Both tests have their own set of proponents and critics.

Theorists have attempted to make IQ testing more objective. The Stanford-Binet test was the first true IQ assessment because it factored in age. The score is based on the test-taker's mental age, as evaluated by the test, divided by the chronological age multiplied by 100.

American psychologist David Wechsler developed three IQ tests; one for preschool and primary children, one for older children and one for adults. The score is based on factor analysis. Sub-tests of the assessment are evaluated against age-based norms.

Another commonly-used test is the Woodcock-Johnson Test of Cognitive Abilities. With the Woodcock-Johnson, extensive tests assess a wide variety of cognitive abilities. All three tests are still in use, and no one test is commonly considered the best or most accurate.

Pros and Cons of Testing

Both EI and IQ testing is controversial. For EI testing, proponents cite that EI helps predict work success and teamwork ability. However, because emotional intelligence runs contrary to the conventional definitions of intelligence, testing is not an accurate predictor of academic or work success. So, while people with high EI do well in the workplace, tests do not necessarily predict who has a high EI. Part of the problem comes in the unreliability of the results. Often, people may not answer accurately because they're trying to do well. Therefore, by definition, the results are subjective.

IQ tests are in regular use in education especially, as well as other industries. Proponents of testing cite that it is a standardized assessment that shows intelligence transcends class, measures the need for special education and measures the effectiveness of special training and programs.

IQ testing can also reveal unsuspected talents. But the limitation of these tests is that they provide limited information. They do not test underlying cognitive processes, nor do they predict success at work because they do not encompass non-academic intellectual abilities. Likewise, original or novel responses get marked as wrong even if they show intelligent thinking. Knowing an IQ score may limit children. Finally, IQ tests may reflect bias against minorities or other cultures with certain types of questions.

Is IQ or EI More Important?

At one point in time, IQ was viewed as the primary determinant of success. People with high IQs were assumed to be destined for a life of accomplishment and achievement and researchers debated whether intelligence was the product of genes or the environment (the old nature versus nurture debate).

However, some critics began to realize that not only was high intelligence no guarantee for success in life, it was also perhaps too narrow a concept to fully encompass the wide range of human abilities and knowledge.

IQ is still recognized as an important element of success, particularly when it comes to academic achievement. People with high IQs typically to do well in school, often earn more money, and tend to be healthier in general. But today experts recognize it is not the only determinate of life success. Instead, it is part of a complex array of influences that includes emotional intelligence among other things.

The concept of emotional intelligence has had a strong impact in a number of areas, including the business world. Many companies now mandate emotional intelligence training and utilize EI tests as part of the hiring process.

Research has found that individuals with strong leadership potential also tend to be more emotionally intelligent, suggesting that a high EI is an important quality for business leaders and managers to have.

For example, one insurance company discovered that EI could play a vital role in sales success. Sales agents who ranked lower on emotional intelligence abilities such as empathy, initiative, and self-confidence were found to sell policies with an average premium of $54,000. For comparison, those agents who ranked highly on measures of EI sold policies worth an average of $114,000.

Emotional abilities can also influence the choices consumers make when confronted with buying decisions. Nobel-prize winning psychologist Daniel Kahneman has found that people would rather deal with a person who they trust and like rather than someone they do not, even if that means paying more for an inferior product.

Can Emotional Intelligence Be Learned?

So you might be wondering if emotional intelligence is so important, can it be taught or strengthened? According to one meta-analysis who looked at the results of social and emotional learning programs, the answer to that question is an unEIuivocal yes.

The study found that approximately 50 percent of kids enrolled in SEL programs had better achievement scores and almost 40 percent showed improved grade-point-averages. These programs were also linked to lowered suspension rates, increased school attendance, and reduced disciplinary problems. Some strategies for teaching emotional intelligence include offering character education, modeling positive behaviors, encouraging people to think about how others are feeling, and finding ways to be more empathetic toward others.

Life success is a result of many factors. Both IQ and EI undoubtedly play roles in influencing your overall success, as well as things such as health, wellness, and happiness. Rather than focusing on which factors might have a more dominant influence, the greatest benefit may lie in learning to improve skills in multiple areas.

In addition to strengthening certain cognitive abilities, such as your memory and mental focus, you can also acquire new social and emotional skills that will serve you well in many different areas of your life.

QUALITIES OF PEOPLE WITH HIGH EMOTIONAL INTELLIGENCE

Have you ever wondered why some people seem to have an unlimited amount of success in both their personal and professional lives? It could be because they possess high emotional intelligence.

"Emotional intelligence is the ability to identify and manage your own emotions and the emotions of others." This usually involves:

If you want to know if you have a high emotional intelligence (EI) or want to work on strengthening your EI in order to succeed in life and your career, here are 10 qualities that people with high EI all share.

1. They're not perfectionists.

Being a perfectionist can get in the way of completing tasks and achieving goals since it can lead to having trouble getting started, procrastinating, and looking for the right answer when there isn't one. This is why people with EI aren't perfectionists. They realize perfection doesn't exist and push forward. If they make a mistake, they'll make adjustments and learn from it. This is one I personally have to work on daily as I tend to be a little more of a perfectionist.

2. They know how to balance work and play.
Working 24/7 and not taking care of yourself adds unnecessary stress and health problems to your life. Because of this, people with EI know when it's time to work and when to play. For example, if they need to disconnect from the world for a couple of hours, or even an entire weekend, they will because they need the time to unplug to reduce the stress levels.

3. They embrace change.
Instead of dreading change, emotionally intelligent people realize change is a part of life. Being afraid of change hinders success, so they adapt to the changes around them and always have a plan in place should any sort of change occur.

4. They don't get easily distracted.
People with high EI have the ability to pay attention to the task at hand and aren't easily distracted by their surroundings, such as text or random thoughts.

5. They're empathetic.
Empathy is one of the five components of emotional intelligence. In fact, being able to relate to others, show compassion, and take the time to help someone are all crucial components of EI. Additionally, being empathic makes people with EI curious about other people and leads them to ask lots of questions whenever they meet someone new.

6. They know their strengths and weaknesses.
Emotionally intelligent people know what they're good at and what they're not so great at. They've not just accepted their strengths and weaknesses; they also know how to leverage their strengths and weaknesses by working with the right people in the right situation.

7. They're self-motivated.

Were you that ambitious and hard-working kid who was motivated to achieve a goal--and not just because there was a reward at the end? Being a real go-getter, even at a young age, is another quality possessed by people with EI.

8. They don't dwell in the past.
People with high EI don't have the time to dwell in the past because they're too busy contemplating the possibilities tomorrow will bring. They don't let past mistakes consume them with negativity. They don't hold grudges. Both add stress and prevent us from moving forward.

9. They focus on the positive.
Emotionally intelligent people would rather devote their time and energy to solving a problem. Instead of harping on the negative, they look at the positive and what they have control over. Furthermore, they also spend their time with other positive people and not the people who constantly complain.

10. They set boundaries.
While people with high EI may seem like pushovers because of their politeness and compassion, they actually have the power to establish boundaries. For example, they know how to say no to others. The reason? It prevents them from getting overwhelmed, burned out, and stressed because they have too many commitments. Instead, they're aware that saying "no" frees them up from completing previous commitments.

SIGNS OF HIGH EMOTIONAL INTELLIGENCE

1. You think about feelings.
Emotional intelligence begins with what is called self- and social awareness, the ability to recognize emotions (and their impact) in both yourself and others.

That awareness begins with reflection. You ask questions like:

- What are my emotional strengths? What are my weaknesses?
- How does my current mood affect my thoughts and decision making?
- What's going on under the surface that influences what others say or do?

Pondering questions like these yield valuable insights that can be used to your advantage.

2. You pause.
The pause is as simple as taking a moment to stop and think before you speak or act. (Easy in theory, difficult in practice.) This can help save you from embarrassing moments or from making commitments too quickly.

In other words, pausing helps you refrain from making a permanent decision based on a temporary emotion.

3. You strive to control your thoughts.
You don't have much control over the emotion you experience in a given moment. But you can control your reaction to those emotions--by focusing on your thoughts. (As it's been said: You can't prevent a bird from landing on your head, but you can keep it from building a nest.)
By striving to control your thoughts, you resist becoming a slave to your emotions, allowing yourself to live in a way that's in harmony with your goals and values.

4. You benefit from criticism.
Nobody enjoys negative feedback. But you know that criticism is a chance to learn, even if it's not delivered in the best way. And even when it's unfounded, it gives you a window into how others think.
When you receive negative feedback, you keep your emotions in check and ask yourself: How can this make me better?

5. You show authenticity.
Authenticity doesn't mean sharing everything about yourself, to everyone, all of the time. It does mean saying what you mean, meaning what you say, and sticking to your values and principles above all else.
You know not everyone will appreciate your sharing your thoughts and feelings. But the ones who matter will.

6. You demonstrate empathy.
The ability to show empathy, which includes understanding others' thoughts and feelings, helps you connect with others. Instead of judging or labeling others, you work hard to see things through their eyes.
Empathy doesn't necessarily mean agreeing with another person's point of view. Rather, it's about striving to understand--which allows you to build deeper, more connected

relationships.

7. You praise others.

All humans crave acknowledgement and appreciation. When you commend others, you satisfy that craving and build trust in the process.

This all begins when you focus on the good in others. Then, by sharing specifically what you appreciate, you inspire them to be the best version of themselves.

8. You give helpful feedback.

Negative feedback has great potential to hurt the feelings of others. Realizing this, you reframe criticism as constructive feedback, so the recipient sees it as helpful instead of harmful.

9. You apologize.

It takes strength and courage to be able to say you're sorry. But doing so demonstrates humility, a quality that will naturally draw others to you.

Emotional intelligence helps you realize that apologizing doesn't always mean you're wrong. It does mean valuing your relationship more than your ego.

10. You forgive and forget.

Hanging on to resentment is like leaving a knife inside a wound. While the offending party moves on with their life, you never give yourself the chance to heal.

When you forgive and forget, you prevent others from holding your emotions hostage--allowing you to move forward.

11. You keep your commitments.

It's common nowadays for people to break an agreement or commitment when they feel like it. Of course, bailing on an evening of Netflix with a friend will cause less harm than breaking a promise to your child or missing a major business deadline.

But when you make a habit of keeping your word--in things big and small--you develop a strong reputation for reliability and trustworthiness.

12. You help others.

One of the greatest ways to positively impact the emotions of others is to help them.

Most people don't really care where you graduated from, or even about your previous accomplishments. But what about the hours you're willing to take out of your schedule to listen or help out? Your readiness to get down in the trenches and work alongside them?

Actions like these build trust and inspire others to follow your lead when it counts.

13. You protect yourself from emotional sabotage.

You realize emotional intelligence also has a dark side--such as when individuals attempt to manipulate others' emotions to promote a personal agenda or for some other selfish cause.

And that's why you continue to sharpen your own emotional intelligence--to protect yourself when they do.

IMPROVING EMOTIONAL INTELLIGENCE (EI)

When it comes to happiness and success in life, emotional intelligence matters just as much as intellectual ability.

Emotional intelligence (otherwise known as emotional quotient or EI) is the ability to understand, use, and manage your own emotions in positive ways to relieve stress, communicate effectively, empathize with others, overcome challenges and defuse conflict. Emotional intelligence helps you build stronger relationships, succeed at school and work, and achieve your career and personal goals. It can also help you to connect with your feelings, turn intention into action, and make informed decisions about what matters most to you.

Emotional intelligence is commonly defined by attributes:

Self-management – You're able to control impulsive feelings and behaviors, manage your emotions in healthy ways, take initiative, follow through on commitments, and adapt to changing circumstances.

Self-awareness – You recognize your own emotions and how they affect your thoughts and behavior. You know your strengths and weaknesses, and have self-confidence.

Social awareness – You have empathy. You can understand the emotions, needs, and concerns of other people, pick up on emotional cues, feel comfortable socially, and recognize the power dynamics in a group or organization.

Relationship management – You know how to develop and maintain good relationships, communicate clearly, inspire and influence others, work well in a team, and manage conflict.

As we know, it's not the smartest people who are the most successful or the most fulfilled in life. You probably know people who are academically brilliant and yet are socially inept and unsuccessful at work or in their personal relationships.

Intellectual ability or your intelligence quotient (IQ) isn't enough on its own to achieve success in life. Yes, your IQ can help you get into college, but it's your EI that will help you manage the stress and emotions when facing your final exams. IQ and EI exist in tandem and are most effective when they build off one another.

Emotional intelligence affects:

Your performance at school or work. High emotional intelligence can help you navigate the social complexities of the workplace, lead and motivate others, and excel in your career. In fact, when it comes to gauging important job candidates, many companies now rate emotional intelligence as important as technical ability and employ EI testing before hiring.

Your physical health. If you're unable to manage your emotions, you are probably not managing your stress either. This can lead to serious health problems. Uncontrolled stress raises blood pressure, suppresses the immune system, increases the risk of heart attacks and strokes, contributes to infertility, and speeds up the aging process. The first step to improving emotional intelligence is to learn how to manage stress.

Your mental health. Uncontrolled emotions and stress can also impact your mental health, making you vulnerable to anxiety and depression. If you are unable to understand, get comfortable with, or manage your emotions, you'll also struggle to form strong relationships. This in turn can leave you feeling lonely and isolated and further exacerbate any mental health problems.

Your relationships. By understanding your emotions and how to control them, you're better able to express how you feel and understand how others are feeling. This allows you to communicate more effectively and forge stronger relationships, both at work and in your personal life.

Your social intelligence. Being in tune with your emotions serves a social purpose, connecting you to other people and the world around you. Social intelligence enables you to recognize friend from foe, measure another person's interest in you, reduce stress, balance your nervous system through social communication, and feel loved and happy.

Building emotional intelligence: key skills to increasing your EI

The skills that make up emotional intelligence can be learned at any time. However, it's important to remember there is a difference between simply learning about EI and applying that knowledge to your life. Just because you know you should do something doesn't mean you will—especially when you become overwhelmed by stress, which can override your best intentions. In order to permanently change behavior in ways that stand up under pressure, you need to learn how to overcome stress in the moment, and in your relationships, in order to remain emotionally aware.

The key skills for building your EI and improving your ability to manage emotions and connect with others are:

- Self-management
- Self-awareness
- Social awareness
- Relationship management

Building emotional intelligence, key skill 1: Self-management

In order for you to engage your EI, you must be able use your emotions to make constructive decisions about your behavior. When you become overly stressed, you can lose control of your emotions and the ability to act thoughtfully and appropriately.

Think about a time when stress overwhelmed you. Was it easy to think clearly or make a rational decision? Probably not. When you become overly stressed, your ability to both think clearly and accurately assess emotions—your own and other people's—becomes compromised.

Emotions are important pieces of information that tell you about yourself and others, but in the face of stress that takes us out of our comfort zone, we can become overwhelmed and lose control of ourselves. With the ability to manage stress and stay emotionally present, you can learn to receive upsetting information without letting it override your thoughts and self-control. You'll be able to make choices that allow you to control impulsive feelings and behaviors, manage your emotions in healthy ways, take initiative, follow through on commitments, and adapt to changing circumstances.

Key skill 2: Self-awareness

Managing stress is just the first step to building emotional intelligence. The science of attachment indicates your current emotional experience is likely a reflection of your early life experience. Your ability to manage core feelings such as anger, sadness, fear, and joy often depends on the quality and consistency of your early life emotional experiences. If your primary caretaker understood and valued your emotions when you were a baby, it's likely your emotions have become valuable assets in adult life. But, if your emotional experiences as an infant were confusing, threatening or painful, it's likely you've tried to distance yourself from your emotions.

But being able to connect to your emotions—having a moment-to-moment connection with your changing emotional experience—is the key to understanding how emotion influences your thoughts and actions.

Do you experience feelings that flow, encountering one emotion after another as your experiences change from moment to moment?

Are your emotions accompanied by physical sensations that you experience in places like your stomach, throat, or chest?

Do you experience individual feelings and emotions, such as anger, sadness, fear, and joy, each of which is evident in subtle facial expressions?

Can you experience intense feelings that are strong enough to capture both your attention and that of others?

Do you pay attention to your emotions? Do they factor into your decision making?

If any of these experiences are unfamiliar, you may have "turned down" or "turned off" your emotions. In order to build EI—and become emotionally healthy—you must reconnect to your core emotions, accept them, and become comfortable with them. You can achieve this through the practice of mindfulness. Mindfulness is the practice of purposely focusing your attention on the present moment—and without judgment. The cultivation of mindfulness has roots in Buddhism, but most religions include some type of similar prayer or meditation technique. Mindfulness helps shift your preoccupation with thought toward an appreciation of the moment, your physical and emotional sensations, and brings a larger perspective on life. Mindfulness calms and focuses you, making you more self-aware in the process.

Developing emotional awareness

It's important that you learn how to manage stress first, so you'll feel more comfortable reconnecting to strong or unpleasant emotions and changing how you experience and respond to your feelings. You can develop your emotional awareness by practicing mindfulness meditation.

Key skill 3: Social awareness

Social awareness enables you to recognize and interpret the mainly nonverbal cues others are constantly using to communicate with you. These cues let you know how others are really feeling, how their emotional state is changing from moment to moment, and what's truly important to them. When groups of people send out similar nonverbal cues, you're able to read and understand the power dynamics and shared emotional experiences of the group. In short, you're empathetic and socially comfortable.

Mindfulness is an ally of emotional and social awareness

To build social awareness, you need to recognize the importance of mindfulness in the social process. After all, you can't pick up on subtle nonverbal cues when you're in your own head, thinking about other things, or simply zoning out on your phone. Social awareness rEIuires your presence in the moment. While many of us pride ourselves on an ability to multitask, this means that you'll miss the subtle emotional shifts taking place in other people that help you fully understand them.

You are actually more likely to further your social goals by setting other thoughts aside and focusing on the interaction itself.

Following the flow of another person's emotional responses is a give-and-take process that rEIuires you to also pay attention to the changes in your own emotional experience.

Paying attention to others doesn't diminish your own self-awareness. By investing the time and effort to really pay attention to others, you'll actually gain insight into your own emotional state as well as your values and beliefs. For example, if you feel discomfort hearing others express certain views; you'll have learned something important about yourself.

Key skill 4: Relationship management

Working well with others is a process that begins with emotional awareness and your ability to recognize and understand what other people are experiencing. Once emotional awareness is in play, you can effectively develop additional social/emotional skills that will make your relationships more effective, fruitful, and fulfilling.

Become aware of how effectively you use nonverbal communication. It's impossible to avoid sending nonverbal messages to others about what you think and feel. The many muscles in the face, especially those around the eyes, nose, mouth and forehead, help you to wordlessly convey your own emotions as well as read other peoples' emotional intent. The emotional part of your brain is always on—and even if you ignore its messages—others won't. Recognizing the nonverbal messages you send to others can play a huge part in improving your relationships.

Use humor and play to relieve stress. Humor, laughter and play are natural antidotes to stress. They lessen your burdens and help you keep things in perspective. Laughter brings your nervous system into balance, reducing stress, calming you down, sharpening your mind and making you more empathic.

Learn to see conflict as an opportunity to grow closer to others. Conflict and disagreements are inevitable in human relationships. Two people can't possibly have the same needs, opinions, and expectations at all times. However, that needn't be a bad thing. Resolving conflict in healthy, constructive ways can strengthen trust between people. When conflict isn't perceived as threatening or punishing, it fosters freedom, creativity, and safety in relationships.

WAYS TO ENHANCE YOUR EMOTIONAL INTELLIGENCE

These days, more and more people are trying to figure out how to improve emotional intelligence. Emotional intelligence refers to the ability of a person to understand and control their emotions. It may not seem like such an important aspect of our life, but it actually plays a very large part in our decision making habits and thinking skills.

People with high emotional intelligence have a much better chance of becoming successful in life, regardless of their IQ. This article will teach you how to improve emotional intelligence. Once you're through reading, you'll have a better grasp of your emotions.

1) R-E-S-P-E-C-T

Respect is not just a seven-letter word in your dictionary. It's a principle you live by. In order to learn how to improve emotional intelligence, you first have to exercise respect for other people's emotions.

When one of your co-workers gets emotional about a personal or professional problem, don't just disregard that person's emotions. Don't start playing loud music just to distract yourself or don't be insensitive to what is going on around you. Instead, give that person your respect through a moment of silence or a look of empathy.

2) Denial is not just a river.

Don't be one of those people who refuse to admit they are in denial. That will just sink you into an even deeper hole than normal.
When you feel sad, angry, dissatisfied, don't tuck those feelings away and try to convince yourself you're happy. Learn to acknowledge your emotions - even the negative ones. As unpleasant as they may be, they will help you mature and will teach you how to improve emotional intelligence.

3) Ear of your heart

When someone tells you to listen with the ear of your heart, it means to show compassion and respect to what other people are telling you. Don't talk too much or interrupt someone who's sharing something about themselves.
By actively listening to what the speaker is saying, you're able to learn twice as much and understand what is really going on.
It's easy enough to learn how to improve emotional intelligence. Knowing the steps is just the beginning. The rest is up to how you apply these tips in your life.

THE PERSONAL BENEFITS OF IMPROVING YOUR EMOTIONAL INTELLIGENCE

Emotional Intelligence (EI) is defined as: The ability to monitor one's own and others' feelings and emotions, to discriminate among them and to use this information to guide one's thinking and actions.

Essentially, EI is a collection of mental and emotional skills. Therefore, to train EI, all you have to do is to train your mind to acquire those skills. Search Inside Yourself, we do that in 3 steps:

Step 1. Attention training. Attention is the basis of all higher cognitive and emotional abilities. Specifically, the idea here is to train attention to create a quality of mind that is calm and clear at the same time. That quality of mind forms the foundation for emotional intelligence.

Step 2. Self-Knowledge and Self-Mastery. Use your sharpened attention to create high-resolution perception into your own cognitive and emotive processes. With that, you become able to observe your thought stream and the process of emotion with high clarity, and to do so objectively from a third-person perspective. Once you can do that, you create the type of deep self-knowledge that eventually enables self-mastery.

Step 3. Creating Pro-social Mental Habits. Qualities such as kindness and compassion can be created as mental habits. E.g., imagine whenever you meet anybody, your habitual, instinctive first thought is, "I wish for this person to be happy." This is the mental habit of kindness and it is highly trainable the same way you train other mental habits.

There are very many benefits to EI. Just in the business world, for example, emotional intelligence has at least three compelling benefits.

First, it is highly correlated with stellar work performance. Studies show emotional competencies to be twice as important as cognitive competencies for doing outstanding work, even among engineers.

Second, emotionally intelligent leaders and managers are far more effective than leaders or managers low on emotional intelligence.

Finally, emotional intelligence create the conditions for personal happiness, and happy workers are a great asset because they work better in teams, provide better service to customers (and happy customers return to spend more money), and are generally more creative and productive.

There are also compelling personal benefits and the most basic of those occur in 3 categories: calmness and clarity of mind, resilience and more satisfying relationships.

First, you become increasingly skillful at calming the body and mind and seeing things clearly and objectively, even in difficult situations. There are studies that show just a few weeks of mindfulness training can reduce the activity of the part of the brain associated with fear panic called the amygdala. There is also a fascinating 2014 study which shows that with merely 15 minutes of mindfulness meditation, you can begin to overcome cognitive bias in decision making.

Second, as you become increasingly skillful at calmness and clarity, you also become increasingly resilient to life's difficulties. Like a kung fu fighter who can defeat more powerful opponents as she becomes more skillful at martial arts, in the same way, you can manage life's problems with increasing ease and joy as your practice gets deeper.

Third, you begin to see yourself with increasing kindness, and you begin to see everyone with increasing kindness, and because of that, relationships become more satisfying. With kindness, happy relationships become happier, neutral relationships become happy, and unhappy relationships become manageable

PRACTICAL WAYS TO IMPROVE YOUR EMOTIONAL INTELLIGENCE

Emotional Intelligence (or EI for short) is a controversial but widely-discussed alternative to traditional IQ. EI measures our ability to perceive our own emotions, as well as the emotions of others, and to manage them in a productive and healthy way.

EI is fundamental to our life experience and can influence how successful we are in our relationships and careers. Whatever stage of life you're at, you can use the seven simple steps below to improve your Emotional Intelligence and develop your self-awareness and empathy.

Practice Observing How You Feel

In the process of rushing from one commitment to the next, meeting deadlines, and responding to external demands, many of us lose touch with our emotions. When we do this, we're far more likely to act unconsciously, and we miss out on the valuable information our emotions contain.

Whenever we have an emotional reaction to something, we're receiving information about a particular situation, person or event. The reaction we experience might be due to the current situation, or it could be the current situation is reminding us of a painful, unprocessed memory.

When we pay attention to how we're feeling, we learn to trust our emotions, and we become far more adept at managing them. If you're feeling out of practice, try the following exercise: Set a timer for various points during the day. When the timer goes off, take a few deep breaths and notice how you're feeling emotionally. Pay attention to where that emotion is showing up as a physical feeling in your body and what the sensation feels like. The more you can practice this, the more it will become second nature.

Pay Attention to How You Behave
As mentioned above, a key part of improving our EI is learning to manage our emotions, which is something we can only do if we're consciously aware of them.

While you're practicing your emotional awareness, pay attention to your behavior too. Notice how you act when you're experiencing certain emotions, and how that affects your day-to-day life. Does it impact your communication with others, your productivity, or your overall sense of well-being?

Once we become more conscious of how we're reacting to our emotions, it's easy to slip into judgment mode and start attaching labels to our behavior. Try to refrain from doing that right now, as you'll be far more likely to be honest with yourself if you're not judging yourself at the same time.

Take Responsibility for Your Feelings and Behavior
This is probably the most challenging step, and it's also the most helpful. Your emotions and behavior come from you—they don't come from anyone else—therefore, you're the one who's responsible for them.

If you feel hurt in response to something someone says or does, and you lash out at them, you're responsible for that. They didn't "make" you lash out (they're not controlling you with puppet strings; after all!), your reaction is your responsibility.

EIually, your feelings can provide you with valuable information about your experience of the other person, as well as your own needs and preferences, but your feelings aren't another person's responsibility.

Once you start accepting responsibility for how you feel and how you behave, this will have a positive impact on all areas of your life.

Practice Responding, Rather than Reacting

There's a subtle but important difference between responding and reacting.

Reacting is an unconscious process where we experience an emotional trigger, and behave in an unconscious way that expresses or relieves that emotion (for example, feeling irritated and snapping at the person who has just interrupted you).

Responding is a conscious process that involves noticing how you feel, then deciding how you want to behave (for example, feeling irritated, explaining to the person how you feel, why this isn't a good time to be interrupting you, and when would be better).

Practice Empathizing with Yourself and Others

Empathy is about understanding why someone feels or behaves in a certain way and being able to communicate that understanding to them. It applies to ourselves and other people, and practicing this ability will improve your EI.

Start by practicing with yourself. When you notice yourself feeling or behaving in a certain way, ask, "Why do I think I'm feeling like this/doing this?" At first, your response might be "I don't know," but keep paying attention to your feelings and behavior, and you'll start to notice different answers coming through.

Create A Positive Environment

As well as practicing the skills mentioned so far (self-awareness, self-responsibility, and empathy), make time to notice what is going well and where you feel grateful in your life.

Creating a positive environment not only improves your quality of life, but it can be contagious to people around you too.

Remember EI is a Lifetime Process

EI isn't something you develop once then drop. It's a lifetime practice, and it is possible to keep improving. Even when you feel like you've mastered these steps, remember to keep practicing, and you'll reap the benefits of EI for the rest of your life.

TIPS FOR IMPROVING YOUR EMOTIONAL INTELLIGENCE

Emotional intelligence fuels your performance both in the workplace and in your personal life, but it starts with you. From your confidence, empathy and optimism to your social skills and self-control, understanding and managing your own emotions can accelerate success in all areas of your life.

No matter what professional field you are in, whether you manage a team of two or 20, or even just yourself, realizing how effective you are at controlling your own emotional energy is a great starting point. Absent from the curriculum, emotional intelligence isn't something we are taught or tested on, so where did it come from, what is it, do you have it and is it really that important?

Put simply, Emotional Intelligence is how well individuals identify and manage their own emotions and react to the emotions of others. It's understanding how those emotions shape your thoughts and actions so you can have greater control over your behavior and develop the skills to manage yourself more effectively. Becoming more emotionally conscious allows us to grow and gain a deeper understanding of who we are, enabling us to communicate better with others and build stronger relationships.

#1) Practice observing how you feel
Often we lead hectic, busy lifestyles and it's all too easy for us to
lose touch with our emotions. To reconnect, try setting a timer
for various points during the day. When the timer goes off, take
a few deep breaths and notice how you're feeling emotionally.
Pay attention to where that emotion is showing up as a physical
feeling in your body and what the sensation feels like. The more
you practice, the more it will become second nature.

#2) Pay attention to how you behave
While you're practicing your emotional awareness, take the time
to notice your behavior too. Observe how you act when you're
experiencing certain emotions, and how that affects your day-
to-day life. Managing our emotions becomes easier once we
become more conscious of how we react to them.

#3) Question your own opinions
In this hyper-connected world, it is easy to fall into an 'opinion
bubble'. This is a state of existence where your own opinions
are constantly re-enforced by people with similar viewpoints.
Take time to read the other side of the story and have your
views challenged (even if you still feel they are right). This will
help you understand other people and be more receptive to new
ideas.

#4) Take responsibility for your feelings
Your emotions and behavior come from you, they don't come
from anyone else and once you start accepting responsibility for
how you feel and how you behave it will have a positive impact
on all areas of your life.

#5) Take time to celebrate the positive
A key part emotional intelligence is celebrating and reflecting on

the positive moments in life. People who experience positive emotions are generally more resilient and more likely to have fulfilling relationships, which will help them move past adversity.

#6) But don't ignore the negative

Reflecting on negative feelings is just as important as reflecting on the positive. Understanding why you feel negative is key to becoming a fully-rounded individual, who is more able to deal with negative issues in the future.

#7) Don't forget to breathe

Life throws various situations our way, with most of us experiencing some sort of stress on a regular basis. To manage your emotions when this happens and to avoid outbursts, don't forget to breathe. Call a time out and go put some cold water on your face, go outside and get some fresh air or make a drink – anything to keep your cool and give yourself a chance to get a hold on what's happening and how you should respond.

#8) A lifetime process

Understand and remember that emotional intelligence is something you develop and requires continual improvement; it's very much a lifetime practice.
Self-awareness
A key component of emotional intelligence, self-awareness is the ability to recognize and understand your own character, moods and emotions and their effect on others. It includes a realistic self-assessment of what you're capable of – your strengths and weaknesses – and knowing how others perceive you. It can help highlight areas for self-improvement, make you better at adapting and can limit wrongful decisions.

#9) Learn to look at yourself objectively

Knowing yourself completely is difficult and it's almost impossible to look at yourself objectively, so input from those who know you is vital. Ask them where your strengths and weaknesses lie, write down what they say and compare it. Look out for any patterns and remember not to argue with them – it doesn't mean they're right – they're just trying to help you gauge your perception from another's point of view.

#10) Keep a diary

A great way to get an accurate gauge of yourself is to keep a diary. Start by writing down what happened to you at the end of every day, how it made you feel and how you dealt with it. Documenting details like these will make you more aware of what you're doing and will highlight where problems might be coming from. Periodically, look back over your comments and take note of any trends.

#11) Understand what motivates you

Everyone has a core motivation when they begin a project. The difficulty is keeping this driving force in mind when adversity appears. All too often people start a project but fail to complete it because they lose their motivation to do so. Take time to understand what motivates you and use it to push you across the finish line.

#12) Take it easy

Sometimes emotional outbreaks occur because we don't take the time out to slow down and process how we're feeling. Give yourself a break and make a conscious effort to meditate, do yoga or read – a little escapism works wonders. And then the next time you have an emotional reaction to something, try to pause before you react.

#13) Acknowledge your emotional triggers

Self-aware individuals are able to recognize their emotions as they occur. It's important to be flexible with your emotions and adapt them to your situation. Don't deny your emotions stage time, but don't be rigid with them either, take the time to process your emotions before communicating them.

#14) Predict how you will feel

Think about a situation you're going into and predict how you will feel. Practice naming and accepting the feelings - naming the feeling puts you in control. Try to choose an appropriate reaction to the feeling rather than just reacting to it.

#15) Trust your intuition

If you are still unsure about which path to take, trust your intuition. After all, your subconscious has been learning which path to take throughout your entire life.
Self-management
Once you've gotten to grips with self-awareness and how your emotions work, you can get a handle on self-management. This means taking responsibility for your own behavior and well-being as well as controlling emotional outbursts.

#16) Snap out of it

One key way to keep your emotions in check is to change your sensory input – motion dictates emotion as the old saying goes. So jolt your physical body out of routine by attending an exercise class or try channeling a busy mind with a puzzle or a book - anything to break your existing routine.

#17) Maintain a schedule (and stick to it!)

Ensuring that you create a schedule and stick to it is extremely important if you want to complete tasks effectively.
"When you schedule appointments in your calendar, you're saying to yourself: "I'm going to do A, B and C by X date and it's going to take Y hours."
Once you make this promise, it becomes harder to procrastinate."

#18) Eat well

This sounds like an easy one but regulating what you eat and drink can have a massive effect on your emotional state, so try your best to maintain a balanced diet.

#19) Don't get mad

Funnel your emotional energy into something productive. It's okay to keep overwhelming emotions inside, especially if it's not an appropriate time to let them out. However, when you do, rather than vent it on something futile, turn it into motivation instead. Don't get mad, get better.

#20) Be interested

A key factor in managing yourself and your emotions is consciously taken the time to be interested in the subject matter, whether it be business or personal.

#21) Don't expect people to trust you (if you can't trust them)

Establishing trust with a person can be difficult, and once it's lost it's very hard to regain. Try to be mindful that people are only human and will make mistakes. By offering your trust, you are inviting people to offer their trust in return.

#22) It's your choice

You have the ability to choose how you react to a situation - you can either overreact or remain calm. But it's your choice.
Motivation
A personal skills aspect of emotional intelligence, self-motivation refers to our inner drive to achieve and improve our commitment to our goals, our readiness to act on opportunities and our overall optimism.

#23) Personal goals

Personal goals can provide long-term direction and short-term motivation. So grab a pen and paper and have a think about where you want to be and set some targets for yourself. Base them on your strengths and make them relevant to you and ultimately, make them exciting and achievable. This task alone is enough to get you instantly motivated!

#24) Be realistic

When you've set a new goal, be sure to give yourself realistic and clear aims to achieving that goal and understand that change is an inevitable part of life. Achievement boosts confidence and as self-confidence rises so does the ability to achieve more, see how it works?

#25) Positive thinking

To keep motivated it's important to maintain a positive and

optimistic mindset. See problems and setbacks as learning opportunities instead of failings and try to avoid negative people and opt to surround yourself with positive, well-motivated people – they'll have a great effect on you.

#26) Lifelong learning

Both knowledge and information are key for feeding your mind and keeping you curious and motivated. And with information so easily accessible, you have the opportunity to fuel your values and passions at the click of a button!

#27) Be prepared to leave your comfort zone

The biggest barrier to achieving your full potential is not challenging yourself frEIuently enough. Great things can happen to you if you're willing to leave your comfort zone, so do so as often as you can.

#28) Help

Don't be afraid to ask for help when you need it, and vice versa. If others need help, don't hold back in giving it to them. Seeing other people succeed will only help to motivate yourself.

#29) Stand and stretch

For an instant short term boost to your motivation, take a stand and stretch out as far as you can for 10 seconds. When you return to your desk, you'll be in the correct frame of mind and ready to work.
Empathy
Quite simply, empathy is the ability to understand other people's emotions. Understanding that everyone has their own set of feelings, desires, triggers and fears. To be empathetic

you're allowing their experiences to resonate with your own in order to respond in an emotionally appropriate way. It's a lifelong skill and the most important one for navigating relationships, and whilst it may not come naturally, there are a few ways it can be nurtured.

#30) Listen

Before you're able to empathize with someone you first need to understand what it is they're saying, which means listening is at the very epicenter of empathy. It involves letting them talk without interruption, preconceptions, scepticism and putting your own issues on pause to allow yourself to absorb their situation and consider how they are feeling before you react.

#31) Try to be approachable

Whether you're the leader of a team or working on a project with others, try to remain accessible and approachable.

#32) Perspective

We're all familiar with the phrase "put yourself in their shoes," and this is exactly that. The simplest way of gaining a little perspective the next time an issue or situation arises is to switch places with the other person and really think about what's happening from their point of view. Sometimes there's no right or wrong, but at least you'll understand enough to come to a resolution or offer some useful advice.

#33) Open yourself up

One of the quickest ways to offer a sincere exchange or sign of empathy is to listen to someone's experiences and connect to it with a similar experience of your own. Don't be afraid to open yourself up, it might just be the start of a great and lasting friendship.

#34) Immerse yourself in a new culture

The old saying 'travel broadens the mind' is still true, even in this ever shrinking world. Sometimes the best way to open your mind is to jump on a plane and go somewhere completely different.

#35) Cultivate a curiosity about strangers

Highly empathetic people have an insatiable curiosity about strangers. When we talk to people outside of our usual social circle we learn about and begin to understand opinions, views and lives that are different to our own. So next time you're sitting on a bus you'll know just what to do…

#36) Acknowledge what people are saying

Another useful tip is, whilst listening to what a person has to say, use acknowledgement words such as 'I understand' and 'I see' to show a person you're listening (but of course only say these things if you are actually listening!).
Social skills
In emotional intelligence terms, social skills refer to the skills needed to handle and influence other people's emotions effectively. It covers a wide range of abilities, from communication and conflict management to dealing with change, meeting new people and building relationships and plays a part in almost every part of our lives, from work life to our romantic life. It's complex and requires utilizing almost every point we have already mentioned, but here are a few pointers for you.

#37) Get started

A good way to get started on improving your social skills is to isolate one skill you know you'd like to develop, this narrows it down and gives you focus. Internationally known psychologist, Daniel Goleman, suggests highlighting someone you know to be good at that particular skill, observing how they act and how they control their emotions and then implementing and applying that knowledge to yourself.

#38) Wear somebody else's shoes

Not literally of course! Everyone has heard the phrase 'walk a mile in somebody else's shoes', but how many people actually practice this advice? Give it a try, you never know.

#39) Practice makes perfect

The idea of practicing your social skills might sound strange, but like everything in life, practice makes perfect.

#40) Social media cold turkey

We don't mean to sound old, but taking your social life offline and engaging face-to-face with people will open up so many opportunities for you to gain and develop your social skills. So next time instead of instant messaging your best friend, meet up for a drink! Emotional intelligence doesn't expand within the confines of (un) social media…

#41) Get networking

A good way to practice your social acumen is to attend local networking events. The great thing about these events is that everyone attending has a shared reason for attending.

#42) It's not what you say, it's how you say it

We're talking about the importance of nonverbal communication and how that can affect a person's opinion of you. Body language, tone of voice and eye contact is key to letting others know how you feel emotionally. So once you've got your emotions intact, think about how you're physically coming across.

#43) The unknown

The ultimate method to building your social skills is to get out there and be sociable. It sounds simple, but you can't strengthen your social skills without being social! Join a group or network outside of your usual circle; it's the perfect way to put all of our tips into play.
What to avoid
Those with a high EI very rarely display the following traits, something for you to be mindful of.

#44) Drama

Emotionally intelligent people listen, offer sound advice and extend empathy to those who need it, but they don't permit others' lives and emotions to effect or rule their own.

#45) Complaining

Complaining implies two things – one, that we are victims, and two, that there are no solutions to our problems. Rarely does an emotionally intelligent person feel victimized, and even more infrEIuently do they feel that a solution is beyond their grasp. So instead of looking for someone or something to blame, they think constructively and dissolve the solution in private.

#46) Negativity

Emotionally intelligent people have the ability to kerb cynical thoughts. They acknowledge that negative thoughts are just that – thoughts – and rely on facts to come to conclusions, as well as being able to silence or zone out any negativity.

#47) Dwelling on the past

Those with high emotional intelligence choose to learn from the mistakes and choices they have made and instead of dwelling on the past are mindful to live in the now.

#48) Selfishness

Whilst a degree of selfishness is rEIuired to get ahead in life, too much can fracture relationships and cause disharmony. Try to avoid being overly selfish and consider others' needs.

#49) Giving in to peer pressure

Just because everyone else does something, they don't feel compelled to follow suit if they don't want to. They think independently, and never conform just to please other people.

#50) Being overly critical

Nothing destroys a person's morale faster than being overly critical. Remember that people are only human and have the same motivations (and limitations) as you. Take the time to understand another person, then communicate the change you want to see.

By understanding and successfully applying emotional intelligence, you too can reach your full potential and achieve your goals.

WAYS TO DEVELOP YOUR EMOTIONAL INTELLIGENCE

Emotional intelligence (EI or EI) is one of the strongest indicators of success in business. Why? EI is not only the ability to identify and manage your own emotions, but it's also the ability to recognize the emotions of others. This study by Johnson & Johnson showed that the highest performers in the workforce were also those who displayed a higher emotional intelligence. And according to Talent Smart, 90% of high performers in the workplace possess high EI, while 80% of low performers have low EI. Simply put, your emotional intelligence matters.

Here are ways to develop your emotional intelligence.

1. Manage your negative emotions. When you're able to manage and reduce your negative emotions, you're less likely to get overwhelmed. Easier said than done, right? Try this: If someone is upsetting you, don't jump to conclusions. Instead, allow yourself to look at the situation in a variety of ways. Try to look at things objectively so you don't get riled up as easily. Practice mindfulness at work, and notice how your perspective changes.

2. Be mindful of your vocabulary. Focus on becoming a stronger communicator in the workplace. Emotionally

intelligent people tend to use more specific words that can help communicate deficiencies, and then they immediately work to address them. Had a bad meeting with your boss? What made it so bad and what can you do to fix it next time? When you can pinpoint what's going on, you have a higher likelihood of addressing the problem, instead of just stewing on it.

3. Practice empathy. Centering on verbal and non-verbal cues can give you invaluable insight into the feelings of your colleagues or clients. Practice focusing on others and walking in their shoes, even if just for a moment. Empathetic statements do not excuse unacceptable behavior, but they help remind you that everyone has their own issues.

4. Know your stressors. Take stock of what stresses you out, and be proactive to have less of it in your life. If you know checking your work email before bed will send you into a tailspin, leave it for the morning. Better yet, leave it for when you arrive at the office.

5. Bounce back from adversity. Everyone encounters challenges. It's how you react to these challenges that either sets you up for success or puts you on the track to full on meltdown mode. You already know positive thinking will take you far. To help you bounce back from adversity, practice optimism instead of complaining. What can you learn from this situation? Ask constructive questions to see what you can take away from the challenge at hand.

Emotional intelligence can evolve over time, as long as you have the desire to increase it. Every person, challenge, or situation faced is a prime learning opportunity to test your EI. It takes practice, but you can start reaping the benefits immediately.

EI AND COMMUNICATION

Our ability to be aware of and understand our own emotions can aid our awareness and understanding of the feelings of others. This sensitivity, or lack thereof, impacts our communication capabilities in both personal and work life.

If we consider communication in the workplace, and more specifically, conflict resolution in the workplace, individuals with higher emotional intelligence are more likely to approach conflict resolution in a collaborative manner, working together with others in order to effectively reach a mutually acceptable outcome.

Relationships in the workplace are affected by how we manage our own emotions and our understanding of the emotions of those around us.

The ability to identify, manage, and understand emotions help us communicate without resorting to confrontation. A person with high EI is better EIuipped to manage conflict and build meaningful relationships given their elevated capacity to understand, and therefore address, the needs of those with whom they engage.

Emotional intelligence has unquestionably received greater attention in recent years as a driver of effective communication within teams, including the growing area of virtual teams (also known as remote or geographically dispersed teams). If we examine EI as a predictor of virtual team success, the results support that not only is EI a driver of team viability, but also positively impacts the quality of communication.

The process of successful communication and, in terms of conflict, successful negotiation are closely linked to high levels of EI. Where those with low levels of EI may react defensively in stressful situations and escalate conflict, individuals with higher emotional intelligence have the skills available at their disposal to communicate effectively without resorting to confrontation or escalating tension.

WHY EMOTIONAL INTELLIGENCE MATTERS FOR HAPPINESS

Happiness seems like a simple enough concept, but have you ever tried to define it? Try now – what is happiness? It is more difficult than it seems because it means something different to each of us. While it is true happiness means distinctly different things to different people, what is clear is emotional intelligence really does matter for happiness irrespective of your interpretation.

EI facilitators such as happiness contribute to our self-actualization and self-actualization, in turn, contributes to our happiness in a positive feedback loop. Happiness is the key factor that has a positive impact on intelligent behavior.

Studies examining the link between EI and a range of interpersonal relations found that participants with higher EI scores had higher scores for empathic perspective taking, self-monitoring and social skills, cooperation with partners, relationship satisfaction, and more affectionate relationships.

By developing the skills for EI one can reduce stress, which consEIuently has a positive impact on well-being and happiness. In addition to its motivational value, happiness monitors one's immediate well-being and interjects positive mood in the way individuals cope with daily demands, challenges, and pressures.

It is this positivity that encourages the emotional energy

rEIuired to increase one's motivational level to get things done, in short, it helps individuals to achieve what they want to achieve and tells them how well they are doing.

Research indicated that a large amount of the variance found in happiness and well-being to be determined by people's emotion-related self-perceptions and dispositions such as the ability to regulate emotions, relationship skills, and social competence.

While these EI skills are not the sole contributor to levels of happiness, it is important to recognize their impact, with over 50% of the total variances in happiness being attributed to emotional intelligence competencies.

From Aristotle to Freud, the emphasis on the optimization of happiness has been thoroughly discussed. To augment happiness one is often rEIuired to use more sophisticated behavioral patterns such as self-regulation to subdue instant pleasure motivations.

Contemporary psychological research continues to recognize the need for this form of optimization. Explicitly taught children how to delay immediate pleasures for greater long-term gain. The ability to delay gratification is important in many aspects of cognitive development given the capacity for such delays encourages an increase in cognitive competence and social maturity.

If we think of happiness in terms of overall life satisfaction, we can agree that developing an aptitude for EI can positively impact well-being and happiness.

STRENGTHS AND EMOTIONAL INTELLIGENCE

The simple premise of the strengths movement came forth from positive psychology. Rather than focusing on your weaknesses, the goal of the movement is to find out what your natural strengths are (and have been from an early age) and develop these further. The central principle is you will get farther faster if you strengthen what you are already naturally good at. Those things you are terrible at doing (and always have been) will never be the areas where you shine. Instead of wasting your time and energy chasing mediocrity, you spend it turning your strongest gifts into greatness.

The simple premise of emotional intelligence came forth from breakthroughs in brain science-specifically, the discovery that the brain is hard-wired to respond emotionally to events before it is able to process things rationally. The goal is to increase your awareness of your emotions so that you can understand them and manage them to your benefit. When you develop self-awareness, you can quit wasting your time attempting to push your emotions aside and allowing them to control you.

Instead, you are able to understand them and manage them to your benefit and the benefit of the people around you. You get farther faster when you become adept at reading emotions and handling them constructively. The best thing about emotional intelligence is it's something you can change. The areas of the brain where emotional intelligence operates are highly elastic-as you develop new behaviors your brain physically changes to make these behaviors into habits that become easier for you to use again in the future.

How Emotional Intelligence Influences Your Strengths:

Every person, no matter their profession or stage in life, should be developing their strengths and their emotional intelligence together in order to make the most out of their opportunities in life. For example, you may discover your strengths include being competitive, strategic, and futuristic; but if you have no self-awareness and no ability to self-manage, you will have a difficult time mobilizing these strengths into personal or professional success.

Picture a true visionary with the motivation to win and the ability to see how to get from here to there. If she's compelled to try to win every conversation with anyone she encounters, she won't recognize when it just may be the worst moment to push too hard and lose the support from key allies she needs to get her vision off the ground. If she lacks the self-awareness needed to understand that she's competing in her conversations, she won't even realize how she's allowing this strength to work against her. The urge to beat others will impede her ability to reach strategic goals and it will slowly erode the quality of relationships that she'll hope to rely upon in the future. If she develops her emotional intelligence skills, she can ensure every interaction with her coworkers will boost her vision and penchant for winning by igniting their support and commitment.

Work on your strengths and EI together:

Strengths and emotional intelligence form a dynamite combination for anyone wanting to differentiate himself in his career. To start, you will want to identify your top five strengths and focus on developing each. Next, measure your current EI skill level, and use the emotional intelligence strategies to help you increase the emotional intelligence skills that you scored lowest on, to raise your overall EI level.

HOW TO EXPLORE YOUR EMOTIONAL INTELLIGENCE

Emotional Intelligence might be described as the ability to control all your emotions and implicitly to exploit wisely your emotional reactions. Also known as, EI, this type of intelligence concerns your social life, because the challenge comes when we are exposed to social factors. Our ability to manage emotions is not necessarily an innate skill; it can be developed and learned so that you will cope successfully with social challenges.

Exploring our emotional intelligence means matching or connecting two different dimensions of self. The inner side encompasses your personal beliefs and set of values, personal long-term goals, whereas, the second dimension concerns the outer world, more precisely, others' emotions, goals, and standards. The way we make connections shows our ability to deal with a wide array of challenges and it might reveal our capacity to readjust our behavior to different inner and external stimuli.

Emotional intelligence is about Equilibrium between inner life and social life. We could benefit from our EI as long as our motivation governing our goals interferes with both plans. A counterbalance between personal and social dimensions brings us closer to the maximum advantage of EI.

We can easily notice if a personal factor has its social

correspondent; therefore, each time we should interrelate socially we are rEIuired to readjust our outcomes to others' values.

Strategies regarding our emotional intelligence are extremely useful in job-related domains or educational realms. Therefore, Neurolinguistic Programming has developed special techniques truly helpful for individuals who are willing to improve their social experiences. EI-driven techniques enable individuals to improve the level of communication and to expand the way they approach difficult issues.

Leadership strategies are based upon the idea that EI can go beyond average communication means and might "manipulate" astutely any audience's perceptions. Leadership is a strategy that involves mainly motivation techniques. In addition to making people trust your assertions, you need to make them adopt a particular behavior.

Exploring our emotional intelligence means developing a particular behavior within a particular context, yet the stress still falls on human factor, because the fundamental purpose of our emotional intelligence relies on others' reactions and feedbacks. Usually, feedbacks stand for a relevant reflection of our emotional intelligence level.

To sum up, emotional intelligence governs our lives since we are involved in a wide array of social activities, and the way we come to benefit from our and others' emotions is definitely a lifetime challenge.

EMOTIONAL INTELLIGENCE AND THE WORKPLACE

Emotional intelligence, sometimes referred to as EI, refers to a person's ability to recognize, understand, manage, and reason with emotions. It is a critical ability when it comes to interpersonal communication—a hot topic not only in psychology, but in the business world. The term itself was coined by psychologists in the 1990s, but its use quickly spread into other areas including business, education, and popular culture.

Psychologists Peter Salovey and John D. Mayer, two of the leading researchers on the topic, define emotional intelligence as the ability to recognize and understand emotions in oneself and others. This ability also involves utilizing this emotional understanding to make decisions, solve problems, and communicate with others.

In the past, emotions and intelligence were often viewed as being in opposition of one another. In recent decades, however, researchers exploring emotion psychology have become increasingly interested in cognition and affect. This area explores how cognitive processes and emotions interact and influence the ways that people think. Consider how emotions and moods such as happiness, anger, fear, and sadness influence how people behave and make decisions.

Studies have shown that employees with higher scores on measures of EI also tend to be rated higher on measures of interpersonal functioning, leadership abilities, and stress management. Other studies have linked higher emotional intelligence with better job satisfaction, as well as overall job performance.

While traditional intelligence was a quality associated with leadership success, it alone was not enough. People who are successful at work aren't just smart - they also have a strong amount of emotional intelligence.

But emotional intelligence is not something just for CEOs and senior managers. It's a quality that is important at every level of a person's career, whether you are a college student looking for an internship or a seasoned employee taking on a leadership role. If you want to succeed in the workplace and move up the career ladder, emotional intelligence is critical to your success.

Why Emotional Intelligence Matters in the Workplace

So why is emotional intelligence such a valued workplace skill? According to one survey of hiring managers, almost 75 percent of respondents suggested they valued an employee's EI more than their IQ.

Some of the reasons why emotional intelligence can be the key to workplace success:

- Emotional intelligence can lead to better business decisions
- Emotionally intelligent employees are more likely to keep their cool under pressure
- Those with high EI are better at resolving conflicts
- Emotionally intelligent leaders tend to have greater empathy

- Employees with high EIs are more likely to listen, reflect, and respond to constructive criticism

Emotional intelligence is widely recognized as a valuable skill, and it is also one researchers believe can be improved with training and practice. While emotional skills may come naturally to some people, there are things anyone can do to help improve their ability to understand and reason with emotions. This can be particularly helpful in the workplace, where relationships and business decisions often rely on interpersonal understanding, teamwork, and communication.

How to Become More Emotionally Intelligent

Since it is such a highly valued skill, is it possible for anyone to have high emotional intelligence? Can people who lack this skill improve their abilities to understand and manage emotions? Factors such as upbringing and personality tend to play a large role in the development of emotional intelligence, but it is a skill that can be improved with effort and practice.

One study found that participants who trained in key emotional competencies not only showed lasting improvements in emotional intelligence, they also experienced improvements in physical and mental well-being, better social relationships, and lower cortisol (stress hormone) levels.

So if you are interested in improving your emotional intelligence skills to benefit your workplace performance, there are a few things you can do.

Become More Self-Aware

One of the first steps toward utilizing emotional intelligence skills in the workplace is to practice recognizing your own emotions. Self-awareness involves being aware of different aspects of yourself, including your emotions and feelings. It is one of the foundational components of emotional intelligence.

In order to recognize your emotions and understand what is causing these feelings, you need to first be self-aware.

Ways to improve self-awareness:

Pay attention to how you are feeling at any given moment throughout the day. How do these emotions influence how you respond? Do the things you are feeling have an impact on the decisions you make or how you interact with others? As you spend more time reflecting on these questions, you may find that you become much more aware of your own emotions and the role they play in your daily life.

Take stock of your emotional strengths and weaknesses. How well do you communicate with others? Do you find yourself experiencing impatience, anger, or annoyance often? What are some ways you can deal with these feelings effectively? Recognizing your weaknesses allows you to look for ways to deal with such shortcomings.

Keep in mind that emotions tend to be fleeting and can change quickly. A co-worker might irritate you or your boss might give you a frustrating task to complete. Before you react, remember these things are temporary, so making rash decisions based on intense emotions can be detrimental to your long-term goals and success.

Practice Self-Regulation

Self-regulation is a critical part of the emotional intelligence. Being aware of your emotions is an important first step, but you also need to be able to manage the things you are feeling. People who possess good self-regulation are able to adapt well to changing situations. They don't bottle things up, but they do wait for appropriate ways to express their emotions rather than just reacting impulsively in the moment. They also think about how their emotional expressions affect others.

Ways to start improving your self-regulation skills in the workplace:

- Find techniques to help you deal with workplace stress. Having hobbies outside of work is a great place to start. Physical exercise is also a healthy way to release stress.
- Keep your cool when things get stressful at work. Accept the fact that you cannot control everything, but look for helpful ways you can respond that don't add fuel to the fire.
- Take time to think before making decisions. Emotions can overwhelm you in the heat of the moment, but you can make a calmer, more rational choice if you give yourself a bit of time to consider all of the possibilities.

Improve Your Social Skills

Research on emotion psychology also suggests people with high EIs also have strong social skills. Because they are adept at recognizing other people's emotions, they are able to respond appropriately to the situation. Social skills are also highly valued in the workplace because they lead to better communication and overall company culture.
Employees and leaders with great social skills are able to build rapport with colleagues and communicate their ideas effectively. People with good social skills are not only great team players; they are able to take on leadership roles when needed.

Ways to strengthen your own social skills in the workplace:

Listen to what others have to say. This doesn't mean just passively listening to other people talk. Active listening involves showing attention, asking questions and providing feedback. Whether you are in a management role or a team member, active listening can show that you are passionate about work projects and willing to work with others to help the group reach its goals.

Pay attention to nonverbal communication. The signals that people send through their body language can convey a lot about what they really think.

Hone your persuasion skills. Being able to carry influence in the workplace and convince team members and supervisors to listen to your ideas can go a long way in advancing your career.

Avoid office drama, but make sure that you are capable of managing conflict. Do your best to stay out of the petty office politics that sometimes take over the workplace, but be aware conflicts are not always avoidable. Focus on listing to what others have to say and look for ways to solve problems and minimize tensions.

Become More Empathetic

Emotionally intelligent people are good at stepping into another person's shoes and understanding how they feel. Empathy is more than just recognizing how others are feeling; it also involves how you respond to these emotions.

In the workplace, empathy allows you to understand different dynamics between colleagues and supervisors. It also allows you to recognize who holds power and how it influences the behaviors, feelings, and interactions that flow from such relationships.

Some ways to work on your empathy in the workplace:

Try seeing things from the other person's point of view. It can be challenging at times, especially if you feel like the other person is wrong. But rather than let disagreements build up into major conflicts, spend time looking at the situation from another's perspective. It can be a great first step toward finding a middle ground between two opposing points of view.

Pay attention to how you respond to others. Do you let them have a chance to share their ideas? Do you acknowledge their input, even if you disagree? Letting others know their efforts have merit often helps everyone feel more willing to compromise.

Work On Your Motivation

Another key component of emotional intelligence is something known as intrinsic motivation. People who have a strong EI tend to be more motivated to achieve goals for their own sake. Rather than seeking external rewards, they want to do things because they find them fulfilling and they are passionate about what they do.

Money, status, and acclaim are great, but people who are highly successful in the workplace are usually motivated by something more than that. They are passionate about what they do. They have a commitment to their work, they love taking on new challenges, and their enthusiasm can seem contagious. They don't give up in the face of obstacles and they are able to inspire others to work hard and persist in order to achieve goals.

Focus on what you love about your job. No matter how you feel about your job, there are probably going to be things about it you love and things about it you hate. In order to build your intrinsic motivation, try focusing on the aspects of your job you truly enjoy. Perhaps you love the feeling of accomplishment you get when you complete a big project. Or maybe you love helping your clients achieve progress toward their own goals. No matter what it is, identify those components of your job and take inspiration from them.

Try to maintain a positive attitude. Notice how optimistic people in the workplace tend to inspire and motivate others as well. Adopting this kind of attitude can help you feel more positively about your work.

Emotional intelligence plays an important role not only in well-being but also in your success in the workplace. Fortunately, there are a number of lessons you can take from emotion psychology that will allow you to improve your EI and foster greater emotional competencies to improve your work performance and career success.

HOW TO USE EMOTIONAL INTELLIGENCE IN THE WORKPLACE

Understanding what emotional intelligence is and why it's so important in the workplace is crucial in today's increasingly competitive world. People are by nature emotional creatures, but only the emotionally intelligent can recognize emotions—both their own and others—and work with them to reach the best possible outcome for everyone. Within the chamber of emotional intelligence lies opportunities to succeed personally and professionally.

The advantages of emotional intelligence at work are many and the organizations that tap into the power of emotional intelligence can set themselves apart from their competition.

These three strategies will set you on the right path.

Prioritize Emotional Intelligence

Contrary to what employees from previous generations may have believed, people can't turn off their emotions when they go to work—nor should they!

The key for business leaders is to strip themselves of preconceived notions about what a boss is supposed to do and approach every situation with a perspective of emotional intelligence. Stomping your feet and yelling at employees to work harder may lead to improved short-term work results, but the long-term effects will almost certainly be disastrous.

Employees today don't necessarily need their boss to be their best friend, but they want a relationship of trust and respect. If they don't get it, they will leave for a manager who gives it to them.

On the flipside, leaders who use emotional intelligence at work to improve relationships will find that their employees are more loyal and perform better. (Not to mention emotional intelligence is connected to better mental and physical health.)

With this in mind, employers should look to hire and promote people who show signs of emotional intelligence, and they should try to help increase the emotional intelligence of their current employees (as we'll discuss below).

However, a word of warning: research shows that a person with more emotional intelligence isn't necessarily more helpful. In other words, when you consider somebody's qualifications for a particular role, emotional intelligence is just one of many factors. Consider this rule-of-thumb:

Skill + Work Ethic + Emotional Intelligence = Successful Professional.

Cultivate a Culture That Encourages Emotional Intelligence

Like any skill, emotional intelligence takes practice. Therefore, organizations should create a culture where employees and managers alike can practice and perfect their emotional intelligence.

The first step is to show your employees that your organization cares. To further explore Carnegie's quote above, your people already understand the logic behind why you want them to perform well: individual success leads to organizational success.

But what about their emotional wellbeing? Do your people know you care about them as individuals, independent of work performance? Once they do, they'll be more likely to follow you.

"If you want to build a ship, don't drum up people to collect wood and don't assign them tasks and work, but rather teach them to long for the endless immensity of the sea." —Antoine de Saint-Exupery

Remember what we said about the ineffectiveness of using threats to get employees to follow? This is especially true when it comes to changing employees' emotional habits. Emotions are stubborn, so you must first help your employees see the vision of why you're asking them to stretch themselves before they'll be willing to do so.

When you gain support on an emotional level, stay at that level. If you return to giving commands after appealing to employee emotions, then the emotional groundwork you've invested in comes across as manipulation instead of caring. Part of true emotional intelligence involves being genuine, and a genuine example of emotional intelligence is much more inspiring than words alone.

Set Goals to Increase Emotional Intelligence

After you've helped your people catch the vision, actively work to increase emotional intelligence among your workforce.

Stress the importance of actions like empathetic communication and open feedback, and then set goals at every level (e.g., organization, department, team, and individual) that can be attached to one of the five emotional intelligence pillars.

Here are some examples of what these goals could look like:

- Identify your emotional triggers and discuss them with your teammates
- Once a month, go to lunch with a coworker who you don't know very well
- Show a willingness to be more approachable by asking a teammate for feedback on a project
- Avoid complaining no matter what for an entire week

After you've set the goals, encourage employees and managers to talk about them. It may seem awkward at first, especially if your people aren't accustomed to open communication, but with practice everyone will get used to it. Steady goal-setting and follow-up to match can lead to greater emotional intelligence.

Conclusion

A lot of this advice is intuitive: Be aware of yourself and others, and treat people with respect. But like anything else, mastering emotional intelligence takes work; that's where so many of us go astray. It's hard to grow emotionally, so we avoid it.

Just remember that practicing emotional intelligence begets more emotional intelligence (just like cognitive intelligence!). And the more emotional intelligence you and your people have, the more likely everyone will succeed.

THE EFFECTS OF LOW EMOTIONAL INTELLIGENCE IN THE WORKPLACE

Low EI can be exhibited in several ways. One of the characteristics of low EI is poor impulse control - the inability to stop, think and decide. Poor impulse control can be evidenced in an employee who reacts to situations without adEIuate consideration instead of planning and preparing for various scenarios. Low EI also causes difficulty managing stressful situations. There are often instances at work that induce stress, and the inability of employees to react in a mature and productive manner could severely damage an organization. Consider the following scenario:

An employee made a bid for a work project and was awarded the assignment. Work begins but the employee begins to feel overwhelmed and no longer desires to complete the project. In a panic, they return the assignment to the manager and rEIuest personal time off of work.

This employee has a low Emotional Intelligence. They also displayed an inability to self-analyze to determine if they were capable of completing the project. They bid on a job impulsively without studying all the circumstances. When in a stressful situation, they chose to react hastily without considering the consEIuences - positive or negative - of their actions.

This type of occurrence can be extremely costly to a business. It could cause loss of clientele, personnel, time and money to reassign the project and meet client specifications.

Low levels of EI also contribute to poor emotional understanding and irrational thinking. Emotions cannot be controlled if they are not first accepted and understood. Under these circumstances employees are not able to view a situation accurately, and particularly not in relation to how it affects others.

Consider this situation:

Two employees are approaching a project deadline, and believe they may not complete the job successfully in the remaining time allotted. They continue to work on the project - missing the deadline - and then turn it in when completed. They did not provide any notice to their superior or to the client.

In this scenario, low EI has again caused the employees to react to situations from an immature view point. They realized they would not meet the deadline, but did not think further about the ramifications for the company. Nor did they seek assistance outside of themselves in order to achieve a successful outcome. Not only would this situation cost the company money, but imagine the work environment that exists if employees do not exhibit concern for their superiors. Interpersonal relationships are guaranteed to be imbalanced and unhealthy.

To correct the effects of low EI in the workplace Cognitive Behavioral Coaching (CBC) has become an increasingly popular practice in businesses. Coaching employees toward Emotional Intelligence through a deep self-awareness that examines beliefs and influences actions reverts the focus of the company from correction to production.

EFFECTIVE LEADERSHIP THROUGH EMOTIONAL INTELLIGENCE

Make no mistake! Leadership styles directly impact employee engagement, culture and business productivity. How long an employee stays and how productive they are is dependent on the relationship they have with their leader.

There is an ongoing challenge for leaders to continually improve productivity and staff retention. This can be achieved by improving engagement of their workforce through Emotional Intelligence. If you emotionally engage workers, they are far more productive.

Emotional Intelligence is about one's ability to perceive, understand, reason with and manage one's own feelings, emotions, mood states and behaviors, as well as those of others. It's your ability that helps people cope with frustrations, control emotions and get along with others.

Our moods, feelings, and emotions influence us every day at work - to a good or bad effect. Not only do they impact every workplace relationship and interaction, they influence fundamental areas like job satisfaction, engagement, and team morale.

Numerous studies have found people high in Emotional Intelligence are happier, healthier and more successful in their business, work and personal relationships.

Start developing your Emotional Intelligence TODAY!

Based on Daniel Goleman's decade of research and model of emotional intelligence, the four (4) main components of emotional intelligence leadership are:

- Self-awareness
- Self-Regulation
- Self-motivation
- Social awareness

1. Self-awareness

Emotional awareness: (Recognizing your emotions and their effects).
- Know which emotions you are feeling and why;
- Understand the links between your feelings and what you think, do, and say
- Recognize how your feelings affect your performance and others;
- Have a guiding awareness of your values and goals.

Accurate self-assessment: (Knowing one's strengths and limits)
- Be aware of your strengths and weaknesses;
- Reflect on and learn from experience;
- Be open to candid feedback, new perspectives, continuous learning and self-development.
- Show a sense of humor and perspective about themselves.

Self-confidence: (Sureness about one's self-worth and capabilities).
- Present yourself with self-assurance; have "presence";
- Voice your views that are unpopular and go out on a limb for what is right;
- Be decisive, able to make sound decisions despite uncertainties

and pressures.

2. Self-Regulation

Self-control: (Managing disruptive emotions and impulses).
- Manage your impulsive feelings and distressing emotions well;
- Stay composed, positive, and unflappable even in trying moments;
- Think clearly and stay focused under pressure.

Trustworthiness: (Maintaining standards of honesty and integrity).
- Act ethically and are above reproach;
- Build trust through their reliability and authenticity;
- Admit your own mistakes and confront unethical actions in others;
- Take tough, principled stands even if they are unpopular.

Conscientiousness: (Taking responsibility for personal performance).
- Meet commitments and keep promises;
- Be organized and careful in your work.

Adaptability: (Flexibility in handling change).
- Smoothly handle multiple demands, shifting priorities, and rapid change;
- Adapt your responses and tactics to fit circumstances;
- Be flexible in how you see events.

Innovation: (Being comfortable with and open to novel ideas and new information).
- Seek out fresh ideas from a wide variety of sources;
- Entertain new solutions to problems;
- Generate new ideas;
- Take fresh perspectives and risks in their thinking.

3. Self-Motivation

Achievement drive: (Striving to improve or meet a standard of excellence).
- Be results-oriented, with a high drive to meet your objectives and standards;
- Set challenging goals and take calculated risks;
- Pursue information to reduce uncertainty and find ways to do better;
- Learn how to improve your performance.

Commitment: (Aligning with the goals of the group or organization).
- Readily make personal or group sacrifices to meet a larger organizational goal;
- Find a sense of purpose in the larger mission;
- Use the group's core values in making decisions and clarifying choices;
- Actively seek out opportunities to fulfill the group's mission.

Initiative: (Readiness to act on opportunities)
- Be ready to seize opportunities;
- Pursue goals beyond what's rEIuired or expected of you;
- Cut through red tape and bend the rules when necessary to get the job done;
- Mobilize others through unusual, enterprising efforts.

Optimism: (Persistence in pursuing goals despite obstacles and setbacks).
- Persist in seeking goals despite obstacles and setbacks;
- Operate from hope of success rather than fear of failure;
- See setbacks as due to manageable circumstance rather than a personal flaw.

4. Social Awareness

Empathy:
(Sensing others' feelings and perspective, and taking an active interest in their concerns)
- Be attentive to emotional cues and listen well;
- Show sensitivity and understand others' perspectives;
- Help out based on understanding other people's needs and feelings.

Developing others:
(Sensing what others need in order to develop, and bolstering their abilities).
- Acknowledge and reward people's strengths, accomplishments, and development;
- Offer prompt and useful feedback and identify people's needs for development;
- Mentor, coach and offer assignments that challenge and grow a person's skills.

Leveraging diversity :(Cultivating opportunities through diverse people).
- Respect and relate well to people from varied backgrounds;
- Understand diverse worldviews and be sensitive to group differences;
- See diversity as opportunity, creating an environment where diverse people can thrive;
- Challenge bias and intolerance.

Political awareness: (Reading a group's emotional currents and power relationships).
- Accurately read key power relationships;
- Understand the forces that shape views and actions of constituents;
- Accurately read situations and organizational and external

realities.

5. Social Skills

Influence: (Wielding effective tactics for persuasion).
- Fine-tune presentations to appeal to the listener;
- Use strategies like indirect influence to build consensus and support;
- Orchestrate dramatic events to effectively make a point.

Communication: (Sending clear and convincing messages)
- You're effective in give-and-take, registering emotional cues in attuning their message;
- Deal with difficult issues straightforwardly;
- Listen well, seek mutual understanding, and welcome sharing of information fully;
- Foster open communication and stay receptive to bad news as well as good.

Leadership: (Inspiring and guiding groups and people)
- Articulate and arouse enthusiasm for a shared vision and mission;
- Step forward to lead as needed, regardless of position;
- Guide the performance of others while holding them accountable;
- Lead by example.

Change catalyst: (Initiating or managing change).
- Recognize the need for change and remove barriers;
- Challenge the status quo to acknowledge the need for change;
- Champion the change and enlist others to pursuit it. Model the change expected of others.

Conflict management: (Negotiating and resolving disagreements).

- Handle difficult people and tense situations with diplomacy and tact;
- Spot potential conflict, bring disagreements into the open, and help de-escalate;
- Encourage debate and open discussion and create win-win solutions

Building bonds: (Nurturing instrumental relationships).
- Cultivate and maintain extensive informal networks;
- Seek out relationships that are mutually beneficial;
- Build rapport and keep others in the loop;
- Make and maintain personal friendships among work associates.

Collaboration and cooperation: (Working with others toward shared goals).
- Balance a focus on task with attention to relationships;
- Collaborate, share plans, information, and resources;
- Promote a friendly and cooperative climate;
- Identify and nurture opportunities for collaboration.

Team capabilities: (Creating group synergy in pursuing collective goals)
- Model team qualities like respect, helpfulness, and cooperation;
- Encourage all members into active and enthusiastic participation;
- Build team identity and commitment;
- Share credit.

Raising emotional awareness takes commitment and practice. Leading with feeling has a Ripple Effect through an entire organization, benefiting everyone through collaboration, greater focus on business objectives, higher performance, and increased bottom-line results.

EMOTIONAL INTELLIGENCE IN THE WORKPLACE - HOW DO YOU MEASURE

Factors are paramount in defining a person's emotional intelligence. These factors can strongly affect your performance at work, how much you enjoy the work you do and how you affect the environment and the people around you.

1. Social Responsibility

In the world of work, we live with other people, people with as many problems and challenges as we do, and who are dealing with them as best they can, just as we are. So when negative things happen at work because of someone else's actions, we can either take it personally and lash out in anger, or try to understand the other person's point of view and respond accordingly.

The latter course helps correct the situation instead of placing the blame, and is the choice of people of high emotional intelligence.

2. Interpersonal Relationships

Are you a giver or a taker? When takers some into conflict, there's no compromise and very little chance of resolution.

Givers rarely come into conflict with one another, but can find themselves in conflict with takers. The taker will take advantage of the finer instincts of the giver, and over time resentment will fester.

Learn to recognize the signs in yourself and those who report to you. If you have control over hiring, hire more giving people. If you have inherited a group of takers, use your communication skills to help them understand and learn to care about the consEIuences of their attitude.

3. Stress Tolerance

You already have a built-in capacity to deal with stress and anxiety, but you can also do a number of things to increase your stress tolerance level.

Learn to recognize the signals in yourself that will let you know when you are about to "lose it" — such as your hands turning into fists or your teeth starting to clench — in time to reverse the reaction. This will help you do some deep breathing or whatever other calming techniques work to reduce your personal stress level.

4. Impulse Control

People with low impulse control can be derailed by e-mail messages, meetings and other situations that can tempt them to react instinctively without engaging their critical thinking mechanism.

People with high emotional intelligence are able to delay their actions or comments until they can be made from a place of intellectual control instead of emotional reaction.

Your emotional intelligence has a huge effect on how you work, how much personal satisfaction you can have in that work and how you contribute to the environment around you.

EMOTIONAL INTELLIGENCE AND RELATIONSHIPS

When we talk about the ingredients for a healthy relationship, we tend to focus on trust, honesty, and communication. And while all these are definitely essential, there is one factor that actually underpins all the others, and often gets lost in the shuffle. I'm talking about emotional intelligence. Why does emotional intelligence matter in a relationship so much? This is so incredibly important in relationships as it helps couples effectively express and manage difficult emotions that arise."

How can you tell if you or your partner are emotionally intelligent? According to the experts, it's all in the way that we communicate with each other. How tapped into the other person's emotions we are and how well we are able to navigate difficult moments and conversations that naturally arise in relationships. While some people are naturally more inclined to emotional intelligence, the good news is it's also a skill that can be learned — one with long-lasting benefits for your happiness and well-being. Here's why the experts say emotional intelligence really does matter.

1. YOU WILL BE ABLE TO EMPATHIZE MORE WITH ONE ANOTHER.

One of the clearest signs of emotional intelligence is empathy, and recognizing and prioritizing the needs of your partner has a huge impact on the health of your relationship. "Empathy rEIuires you to postpone your agenda and really tune into to what someone else is feeling and to understand those feelings." We all want to be seen and understood, and having a partner that is tuned into us, and vice versa, is a way to forge and deepen your bond.

2. YOU CAN HAVE A CRITICAL CONVERSATION WITHOUT IT ESCALATING.

People who are emotionally intelligent are capable of receiving criticism well. Why that matters in a relationship is that sometimes, constructive criticism is necessary, and if it isn't received or it escalates into a fight then it shuts down important communication. "Being open to criticism shows that you're open to learning and growing." "Instead of feeling attacked or blamed, you view it as an opportunity to learn and understand which helps you to keep your emotions in check."

3. YOU'RE ABLE TO BE FULLY VULNERABLE WITH ONE ANOTHER.

It's not easy to be vulnerable with other people, but in order to really connect with your partner you have to be able to drop your guard. Knowing how and when to do so is all a part of emotional intelligence, as well as recognizing the reasons why you may be holding back. "If a partner is able to identify a pattern in which they feel an emotion that makes them vulnerable and expresses that to you, they demonstrate emotional intelligence and a pulse on the relationship."

4. YOU WILL BE MORE ABLE TO EXPRESS YOUR FEELINGS DIRECTLY.

Being passive aggressive or using the silent treatment to manage conflict are signs of a lack of emotional intelligence — but there's also a flipside. "A partner who is emotionally intelligent is verbally expressive and says what they mean and how they feel — respectfully." This is important because speaking up is the only way to have your needs properly met. "An unexpressed need is an unmet need so being able to authentically share how you feel and ask for what you need from your partner is incredibly powerful in a relationship."

5. YOU WILL BE ABLE TO APOLOGIZE TO EACH OTHER AND MAKE UP MORE QUICKLY.

It can be hard to swallow your pride and admit you are wrong after an argument, but the ability to do so is a clear sign of emotional intelligence, and how you keep resentment from building up and poisoning the relationship. "[An emotionally intelligent partner is] quicker to apologize for wrongdoing." "They desire to maintain connection and are more intuitive about their part in creating the distance. They recognize and take ownership and seek to make amends ... They would rather be close than right."

Ultimately, emotional intelligence matters because it breaks down barriers between you and you partner and allows you to understand one another. It also means the difference between a productive argument that brings you closer together, and a fight that escalates and eventually ends the relationship. I think we can all agree it's a pretty big deal, and an important aspect of any relationship that deserves attention and nurturing.

EMOTIONAL INTELLIGENCE AND ITS ROLE IN PERSONAL RELATIONSHIPS

Emotional Intelligence (EI) is the ability within a person to control and perceive emotions. It therefore happens to play an extremely important role in the relationships, one makes and breaks, during the course of his or her lifetime.

Relationships may develop when two people find each other interesting, have something in common or just enjoy each other's company. For a relationship to be strong and last longer there has to be some level of emotional attachment between those in that particular relationship. It can be observed in daily life with ease that those relationships without any emotional attachment and understanding and those with stakes, cease to exist. Understanding is therefore vital in any relationship. This comes with emotional intelligence.

With emotional intelligence, a person can understand the other and he can perceive his emotions and feelings. In every instant, he would know what to say and what to do which would bring up the morale of the other person and not make him disappointed or sad. If things go wrong, the person would know how to react and resolve things in a way nobody gets hurt.

Communication, too, is Equally important in long-lasting relationships. Communication does not only refer to speaking.

It does not only mean to say the right things at the right times, but also to stay silent and listen to the other person when need be. A good communicator will judge the mood and emotions of the other person and act accordingly, bringing emotional intelligence into play.

Somebody with a high emotional intelligence will always have an edge in his personal relationships compared to a person with lower emotional intelligence. A good level of communication determines how the relationship will continue and for how long. In every relationship, whether it is friendship or marriage, communication is critical, not to mention the importance of communication in business organizations.

Patience and managing stress well help a relationship work for longer. As when one person is not happy with the way things are going the other, understanding how he might be feeling should act accordingly and help him come out of that situation for a better and stronger relationship.

In fact, if people in relationships do not have emotional intelligence, their relationship would not last too long and it would be very dry. They would not understand each other on any matter. The person would be without any feelings for the other and without any sense of keeping relationships.

WAYS THAT EMOTIONAL INTELLIGENCE CAN MAKE YOU BETTER AT EVERYTHING

Many of us are missing out when it comes to another essential form of intelligence. Yes, we're talking about emotional intelligence (EI), the ability to understand your emotions and those of others, while effectively regulating the former in tandem. This set of skills can be a serious game-changer in virtually every part of your life, of course, but perhaps none more so than in an inter-relationship capacity.

What we're trying to say is, whether you're trying to be a more sympathetic spouse, an easier roommate to live with, or a monk-level patient parent, EI can change your relationships for the better in no time. And luckily, even if you haven't always been emotionally available in the past, it's never, ever too late to start.

It Makes You a Better Listener

In romantic relationships, being a good listener can mean the difference between staying in love for the long run or becoming mutually resentful of one another. Fortunately, by being in tune with your emotions and understanding the emotional needs of your partner, being an active, receptive listener is simple. Think listening's not that big a deal? Think again: researchers found that people whose partners were good listeners had less physiological stress and improved emotional states.

It Makes You More Open to Change

The one constant in most relationships is change: you're likely to change careers, homes, and personality ticks—not to mention hairstyles—over the course of a long-term relationship. Luckily, for emotionally intelligent people who can anticipate and understand these changes in both themselves and their partners, it's easier to embrace these new developments in your relationship, instead of running from them.

It Helps You See Things From Their Perspective

One major factor that predicts the long-term success of a relationship is the ability to empathize with your partner and see things from their point of view. Fortunately, emotionally intelligent people have honed their knack for expressing empathy for others, making it easier to understand a partner's feelings, even if they don't share them.

It Can Help You Anticipate Your Partner's Needs

Knowing what your partner needs before they even ask can serve you well in a relationship, whether you're giving them a shoulder to cry on or just picking up the right sushi rolls on the way home from work. The good news? Emotionally intelligent people are particularly adept at this skill.
"EI helps you predict your loved one's needs and wants more accurately". "You will be more likely to get just the right gift or say just the right thing to comfort them when they are having a hard time."

It Helps You Accept Criticism

For a relationship to stay healthy, both partners need to grow together, which often means learning both what your partner already loves about you and what they think you could stand to work on. If you're emotionally intelligent, or are working on honing those skills, it's easy to accept constructive feedback from your partner and make the appropriate changes without getting defensive or taking things personally.

It Makes You Focus on Your Priorities

With work and other commitments encroaching on your relationships, it's easy to lose sight of the life you're eager to have with your partner. However, for those with practiced emotional intelligence, recognizing what you value in your relationship and carving out time to prioritize your partner will feel like a healthy—and easy—choice.

It Increases Your Emotional Availability

If you want to be the kind of partner your significant other always feels like they can open up to, it's time to start working on your emotional intelligence now. Being emotionally intelligent means you're attuned to both your emotional needs and those of your partner, making it easier for them to come to you when they need guidance or support.

It Helps You Roll With the Punches

Every relationship has its difficult times, and in many cases, they're impossible to see coming. However, for those with high levels of emotional intelligence, instead of running away when the going gets tough, they realize making things work with someone they love is well worth weathering the ups and downs.

It Helps You See The Good in One Another

It's pretty easy to start taking someone for granted after you've been together for a long time. If you're particularly emotionally intelligent, however, it's easier to recognize when you're not appreciating your partner as much as you should, and correct your behavior to remedy this misstep. EI also helps you recognize when your partner has unintentionally acted in error or taken you for granted, instead of assuming they're doing things a certain way to upset you.

"EI helps you give your loved ones the benefit of the doubt in ambiguous interactions. For example, you may have asked your spouse to get you your favorite kind of tea at the grocery store. He or she comes back with a different kind of tea. It may be easy to assume your spouse just didn't care enough to get the right thing and then tell them how that hurts your feelings, and then get into an argument about it. Being able to give your spouse the benefit of the doubt may lead you to think that the store may have been out of your favorite kind of tea, but he/she did their best to get you something you'll like almost as much. And the outcome of this interaction would be quite different."

It Helps You Stay Committed

While even the healthiest relationships wax and wane, there's one factor all long-term relationships have in common: people staying committed to them. If you're emotionally intelligent, understanding how devastating the loss of fidelity or partnership would be to your significant other can help you stay emotionally invested in the long run. In fact, one study revealed emotional intelligence accounted for more than 40 percent of overall marital satisfaction among couples studied.

It Can Help You Get the Things You Ask For

For roommates, emotional intelligence is surprisingly important, as well. While many roommates find themselves at odds when they assume the people they live with will anticipate their needs, emotional intelligence can make you a better communicator, thus making it easier to make your needs known and get them met.

"EI helps you to ask for what you need with a higher likelihood of success." "Let's say your roommate has been very loud early in the morning, slamming doors and stomping around, waking you up and disturbing your sleep. You could yell at them, tell them to stop being a jerk and let you sleep. This is unlikely to make your roommate be quieter. Or you could say something like: 'I know you've had to wake up earlier lately, and it must be hard to be up so early! I've been able to hear you getting ready in the morning, and it's been hard for me to sleep, too. Could you pay a little more attention to being quiet in the morning?' This request is more likely to get your needs met."

It Makes Compromise Easier

Compromise is key when it comes to getting along with your roommate. Fortunately, for those with high emotional intelligence quotients, coming to a compromise, whether it's about whose job it is to unload the dishwasher or where to put the sofa in the living room, is not such a big deal. For emotionally intelligent people, it's easy to understand your roommate's perspective and weigh it carefully against yours, rather than simply assuming you're right.

It Makes You More Respectful

Disrespectful behavior can turn a happy roommate situation into a contentious one in a hurry. If you get lucky and find yourself living with someone with a high degree of emotional intelligence, however, odds are you won't find them borrowing your things without asking or leaving the place a mess.

It Helps You Recognize Other People's Motivations

Sometimes, inconsiderate behavior is worth arguing with your roommate over. And sometimes, it's better just to fix things and have a healthy talk about it afterward. Emotionally intelligent people tend to know the difference between a roommate who left a dish in the sink when they were in a rush and one who intentionally left it there because they were thoughtless or wanted to upset you.

"EI helps you understand where the other person is coming from, and helps you interpret their words and actions more accurately." "This way you are less likely to assume a negative intention on the part of the others person and blame them for it."

It Makes You Better at Sharing

While it's nice to imagine that everyone has mastered sharing by the time they finish preschool, that's often far from the case. In roommate situations, it can be difficult to share your space and things with another person, but emotional intelligence can help. Understanding that your roommate's needs are just as important as your own and recognizing why they might want to commandeer the living room for an evening when you had friends over the night before can help you get better at sharing.

It Makes You More Mindful

Being mindful is key to having a healthy roommate relationship, but it's a skill that often gets overlooked. Fortunately, emotional intelligence and mindfulness have a symbiotic relationship. Not sure how that works? Emotional intelligence can help a person recognize what the outcome of slamming a door or screaming might be, and weigh it against the impact of having a calm conversation with the person who might be making them irate. In turn, mindful and emotionally intelligent people will make the choice that benefits the relationship in the long run rather than the one that feels good in the moment.

It Makes You Less Codependent

Roommate codependency is very real, and can have a detrimental effect on even the tightest roommate pairs over time. If you're looking to reduce codependency issues in your roommate relationship, start by working on your emotional intelligence. When you realize the strain serious codependence can take on your relationship, you'll loosen your grasp. Better yet, emotional intelligence makes it easier to find contentment, even if you're alone.

It Reduces Passive-Aggressive Behavior

Passive-aggressive behavior can quickly put a damper on any roommate relationship. The good news? Emotionally intelligent people don't resort to being passive-aggressive to get their point across: they simply say let other people know what they need, and respect the needs of others, in return.

It Makes You More Thoughtful

Much like in a romantic relationship, a little thoughtfulness can go a long way when it comes to keeping things amicable between roommates. For those who are emotionally intelligent, the idea of cooking dinner, cleaning up the house, or doing other thoughtful things for their roommates comes naturally, knowing they'll keep the relationship happier in the long run.

It Helps You Resolve Conflict More Peacefully

Of course, even the closet roommates do get into fights from time to time. The good news for those with adEIuate emotional intelligence, however, is that prioritizing effective, kind resolution of conflict trumps winning an argument, and that, in turn, helps keep things civil and maintains the relationship for the long haul.

It Makes You More Patient

For parents, emotional intelligence can have profound effects on your patience. While parents with low emotional intelligence quotients often subconsciously prioritize their needs over those of their children, emotionally intelligent parents will take the opposite approach. Instead of assuming their children will have adult-level skills or abilities, emotionally intelligent parents realize their kids do things differently, and sometimes in ways that can be frustrating, and understand that's okay.

It Helps You See Their Perspective

Kids and adults don't always see eye-to-eye. Fortunately, for parents with ample emotional intelligence, it's easy to empathize with your kids' struggles and see where they're coming from. In turn, this may have a cyclical effect: in fact, one study reveals that parental emotional intelligence was a good predictor of a child's behavior in stressful circumstances, too.

It Helps You Keep Your Cool

It's easy to lose your cool when your kids are being terrors. However, parents with ample emotional intelligence can accurately weigh the impact that yelling or inappropriately punishing their children will have versus having a calm conversation with them, and will overwhelmingly choose the latter.

It Keeps You From Projecting

It's often hard to recognize your own feelings as distinct from those of your children as a parent, but doing so is important to the health and success of your relationship. Research suggests that low emotional intelligence is correlated with low self-awareness, which can sometimes translate to an inability to distinguish what you're feeling from feelings you're attributing to your kids. Fortunately, trying to hone your emotional intelligence skills can help you recognize when it's your own emotions ruling the show, and not the behavior or feelings you're attributing to your kids.

It Helps You Realize When They Need Help

It's to be expected that not all children will have the same capability for emotional intelligence as adults. However, that's why it's so important for parents to be emotionally attuned—it can help parents realize when their kids need help, but aren't asking for it, and respond appropriately.

It Increases Your Confidence

Being a parent means being a leader in your family, and there's no such thing as effective leadership without confidence. Fortunately, being emotionally intelligent is associated with high self-confidence, which can help you stick to your guns about your parenting decisions, raising healthier, more disciplined kids along the way.

It Makes You Easier to Open Up To

Emotionally intelligent parents know that their children's emotional needs come before their own. And if your kids aren't worried their emotional outpouring will be met with one of yours in return, it will be a lot easier for them to open up.

It Helps You Mediate Sibling Rivalry

Sibling rivalry is a natural part of many sibling relationships, but luckily, emotionally intelligent parents have the skills needed to mediate it. By understanding when it's important to step in, when it's a good idea to let your kids figure things out on their own, and how to remain impartial when discussing their issues with them, it's easy to help your kids work things out.

It Helps You Celebrate Their Successes

While some parents can feel threatened by their kids' successes, emotionally intelligent ones know how to celebrate the victories of the people they love. Recognizing your kids' victories as their own, instead of reflections upon you, will help you feel happy when they succeed instead of being resentful.

It Makes You a Better Role Model

Overall, emotionally intelligent parents are better role models than those who are closed off or unkind. When you think of how you want your children to behave as adults, don't you want them to be nurturing, loving, and open to new ideas? Luckily, modeling emotional intelligence today can help set them on that healthy course for tomorrow.

HOW TO RAISE YOUR EMOTIONAL INTELLIGENCE

In order to raise your Emotional Intelligence level, you must become self-aware of the emotions that you are experiencing at any given time, and you must also deal with emotions you have suppressed in an effort to avoid dealing with them. It is a common tendency to want to push down a certain emotion or to convince yourself you are not experiencing a particular emotion because it is uncomfortable or for some reason that emotion seems inappropriate under the circumstances. Emotional Intelligence rEIuires you know your own emotions and you know how to manage them.

This is not something that you are able to do automatically - it is a process. In order to successfully complete this process, it will help to remember the following facts about your emotions:

Emotional intelligence is based on emotional awareness

Emotional Intelligence differs from regular or classic intelligence in that you can raise your Emotional Intelligence practically at will. And being emotionally intelligent is a crucial part of building solid relationships with family, friends and co-workers. People with high Emotional Intelligence are appreciated because they are steady, calm, collected, and secure, and they seem to have an innate ability to understand others.

They always seem to know what to do in any given situation because their emotions don't overwhelm them, so they are able to think more clearly and act more reasonably.

Emotions are constantly changing

Becoming self-aware of your emotions and what triggers them is not the same as dwelling on them. Take note of how the different things you do on any given day cause one emotion to arise and another to subside and you'll see emotions are always subject to change.

Your emotions are often tied to physical sensation

You've probably noticed the way your body reacts to the emotion of fear is different from the emotion of happiness, the way you feel physically when you're happy is different from when you are angry, and so on. For instance, paying attention to the fact your hands are shaking, that your muscles are tense and that your heart is beating rapidly, all of which are tied to being afraid, will help you realize why you are afraid and will help you manage that fear, so you can handle it constructively.

Emotional Intelligence doesn't replace reason & logic

Becoming aware of what emotions and feelings you are experiencing and knowing how to manage those emotions and feelings will become essentially automatic. Once you no longer struggle to deal with your emotions and feelings instinctively, your thinking and reasoning abilities are clearer and more accurate, and you can use them to work through your emotions without being overcome by them. Just like anything else, you will become better at this as you practice, practice, practice.

When we have an understanding of our emotions, what they

are, and how they affect us we are building the foundation to being self - aware. Self management then follows with a differing set of competencies taking us further down the path of raising our emotional intelligence.

THE SECRETS TO USING EMOTIONAL INTELLIGENCE TO GET AHEAD IN LIFE

The term, "emotional Intelligence" refers to the ability to asses, identify and control your emotions or that of others or groups. The process can be acquired through learning although it can also be in born in some individuals. You can actually use emotional intelligence to get ahead in life if you care to know the secrets involved in using it.

The secrets you have to know are mainly hidden in the four branches of emotional intelligence. Let's take a look at them.

• Perceiving Emotions

Learning how to perceive emotions is the first secret you need to discover. This might require the understanding of nonverbal signals such as facial expressions and body language. You have to perceive emotions through such signals in order to get ahead to the next level of life.

• Reasoning with Emotions

This is yet another secret you need to know about using emotional intelligence. This involves the use of emotions to promote cognitive and thinking activities. You can reason out with emotions to know issues you have to pay attention to. You can equally reason out how you can respond to issues emotionally in order to garner the required attention. Reasoning with emotions also involves your brain and thinking faculty. Your ability to develop your mind power can actually help you a lot in the reasoning process.

• Understanding Emotions

This is another vital secret you need to know about using emotions. You have to discover how best to understand the emotions you're having. Oftentimes, the emotions one expresses carry along deep or wider meanings. If for instance, you're hurt, someone who understands emotions can easily decode that and also interpret the cause of your hurt. Again, if your loved one is angry, you can easily read meaning into the emotion he or she portrays and then interpret the cause of the anger.

• Managing Emotions

This is perhaps the greatest secret you need to discover in order to ahead in life. Many people fail at this point. They find it difficult to manage their emotions especially when they are angry. If you're not able to manage your emotions when you're angry, you can easily strike someone dead with a weapon only to regret it afterwards when your emotions are gone.
Indeed, the ability to manage your emotions is the major key in emotional intelligence. You have to practice how to control your emotions in order to get ahead in life.

The following tips can help you use emotional intelligence properly
• Decode your feeling

- Share your feeling with others
- Learn to understand others' feelings
- Learn to tolerate others when they react
- Think of various options when you're faced with a decision
- Marshall out realistic life goals and try to pursue them
- Use the power of positive thinking to fight bad emotions

With these secrets and tips discussed above, you can always discover how to use emotional intelligence to get ahead in life. There's every need to put the secrets you learn into practice. The more you practice, the easy it becomes for you to use the techniques discussed.

CPSIA information can be obtained
at www.ICGtesting.com
Printed in the USA
LVHW051433260420
654439LV00004B/1174